T0383522

marcel DZAMA

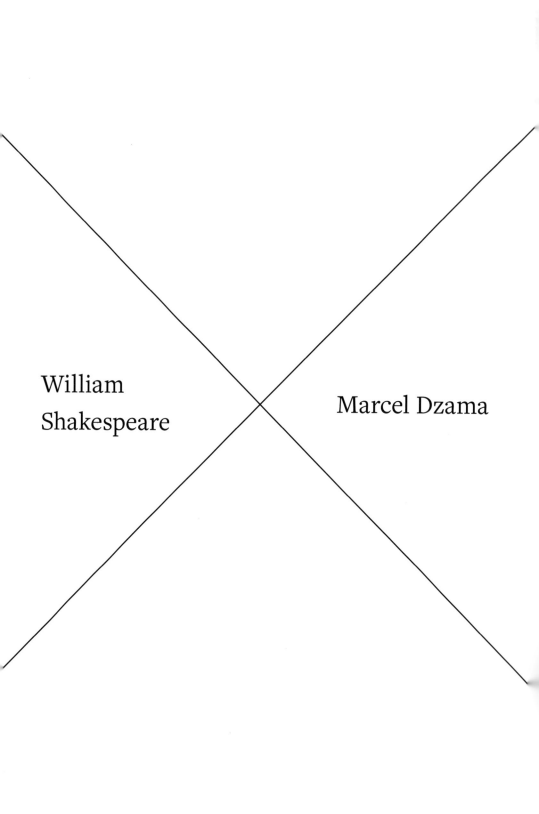

William
Shakespeare

Marcel Dzama

A Midsummer Night's Dream

By William Shakespeare
With a text by Leslie Jamison
Artwork by Marcel Dzama

David Zwirner Books

marcel DZAMA

Sympathetic Magic: On Love, Ritual, and the Dream of Midsummer

Leslie Jamison

The summer solstice is the longest day of the year, which means it marks the year's turn toward darkness. Its brightness holds the promise of expanding night. It is the same with bliss, I think: when we feel happiest, we know it won't stay this way forever. All the light-swollen hours hold the prospect of their own unraveling. Every joy is already grieving its own disappearance.

The summer solstice was traditionally celebrated with fire: villagers jumping through the flickering flames of a bonfire, or passing their milk cows through the smoke. *Bonfire* comes from *bone fire*, a fire of animal bones burned to ward off evil spirits. The solstice was a night when the boundary grew porous between the world of spirits and the world of ordinary mortals, when the business of daily living brushed up against the great shimmering veil of whatever lived in the smoke. The communal bonfire was a form of sympathetic magic—the fire meant to represent the sun, its surging flames meant to coax the light to stick around for the months of growing and harvesting that lay ahead. The bonfire was a way of saying, *We know you'll leave. But leave slowly.* As we might say to our joy at its peak, *Stay a little bit longer?*

I was born on the summer solstice, which was also the first day of summer vacation for my two older brothers. A good omen, they told me later. All my birthdays have been limned by the bright lines of late dusk: childhood sleepovers when my friends and I lay in my living room like sardines, shoulder to shoulder in our sleeping bags, whispering until the tides of tiredness carried us into sleep; or sitting on the wooden deck of a lifeguard station with my high school boyfriend, feeling his hands under my shirt as the sun finally dipped into the sea, streaking red across the sky. Like all birthdays, mine has often felt charged with portent, its events like tea leaves, holding the future in their spread—but in my case they've been lit by a stubborn sun, encased by a sense of extremity and imminent diminishment.

On my last birthday, my best friend and my toddler daughter and I drove to a cottage in the rural Catskills. On a shadowy road our rental car was flagged down by a group of Orthodox Jewish men who asked me to come with them to their cabin in the woods—they needed me to turn on the lights for them, they said. It was a Friday night, the Sabbath. Their cabin was set back from the road, in the black webbing of the trees. I'd been a woman for many years, and of course I knew it probably wasn't a good idea to let a group of strange men take me deep into the dark woods. And yet, my gut told me they just wanted the light. It was as if I could see two different stories splitting off from that roadside: one was violent, the other like a dream; and these stories flickered side by side, like two worlds whose dividing boundary had grown porous. And when I finally followed the men—through the trees, back to their wooden cabin— and flipped the switch, the story came into focus. We were flooded with fluorescent light.

A decade earlier, I spent my twenty-sixth birthday with the man I thought I would spend my life with. We ate melon wrapped in prosciutto on a balcony jutting out between the crooked teeth of pastel houses in an Italian town called Riomaggiore. We were watching the sun set over the sea—late, late, late, the sky pink and blue, the light still as stubborn as it had been for me at sixteen. We had a cold bottle of cheap white wine, sweating all over its curves; we had creamy Taleggio that could barely keep its shape; we had our bathing suits on. We had such sublime faith, untainted by life. We believed that if you loved someone this much, you could make that person happy. We believed in the long days and the late light and the cheap wine and the good cheese and the deep lust and the lilting music from a stone church coming to us on the salt breeze. We stripped naked and slow-danced in the night. It was like that.

A few months after that relationship ended, I got naked on another summer solstice. I was turning thirty, recently tattooed, about to move to New York. I was staying with a friend down in Baltimore, where her parents' house had a swimming pool beneath a rustling canopy of trees. In the darkness our bodies made tiny splashes and moonlit ripples across the chlorinated water. Out there, naked in the darkness, I felt that shivery membrane between worlds getting patchy and porous—the boundary between what I'd already lived and what I thought might be possible. There was the landscape of my days—covering my Vaseline-slicked tattoo in plastic wrap, renting a U-Haul to drive my boxes to Brooklyn—and then there was this humid, unreal night: the blue glow of the water, its silken weight clasping and unclasping as my limbs slipped through it. The moon was waxing gibbous that night, just a day from full. The Strawberry Moon of June. The supermoon of the year. The moon at perigee, closer to Earth than it would be at any other moment. Everything was unknown and close enough to touch. All my possible lives stretched like forking paths through the darkness.

I had no idea what lay ahead, swimming naked under the light of an almost supermoon, after the end of the longest day of the year, when the forces of mischief and destiny were making plans for me that I knew nothing about. I might have guessed the nouns—marriage and leases and classrooms and plane flights—but not their arrangement, and certainly not all the pit stops on their highway: bitter fights without trapdoors, my water breaking in the middle of the night—after a blizzard, in the dead of winter—and contractions in a cab on the highway by the East River, and signing divorce papers on Valentine's Day, and a toddler giving little popping kisses to her stuffed flamingo, and a dark room lit up suddenly in the dark woods upstate, just me and the Orthodox strangers, gathered for the miracle.

Sometimes it feels as if the world is whispering in your ear, telling you that you're not in control, that you never were—that all your possible lives are glimmering on the other side of the thinnest membrane, and things are going to get stranger and harder and more sublime than you've ever imagined.

✳

The first time I saw a production of *A Midsummer Night's Dream* I was four years old and thrilled by the gold glitter tossed from the stage at the end of Puck's epilogue. He told us everything had been a dream—"That you have but slumbered here / While these visions did appear"—and then the sparkling confetti surrounded us. "No more yielding but a dream," Puck said, but the glitter was something I could touch. It was in my hair. It was all over my skin. It was like waking up from a dream about the ocean to find my clothes damp, my hair caked in salt.

This was a high school play, and my older brother was a freshman doing tech backstage. I worshipped anything he was involved in, but I think I would have worshipped that play anyway—just for the glitter at the end, like the splash zone at a dolphin show: best seats in the house. You wanted to get wet with the show. Feel marked by it.

What did I understand about *Midsummer* at four? That it was full of fairies. That it took place in an enchanted forest. That the characters' speeches didn't make much sense but often rhymed. That we all sparkled at the end!

And in a way, this is *exactly* what the play is about: events that glitter with possibility and danger and wonder, but don't entirely make sense. Even for the overly cerebral, love-hungry college sophomore I would eventually become, poring over the *Midsummer* footnotes fifteen years later. Another fifteen years after *that*, the play still strikes me as being fundamentally about the experience of coming up against something you don't entirely understand: a story, an emotion, a love affair. It offers a vision of life as a cosmic unfolding of dramatic action written by a mysterious stranger who has no intention of explaining anything to you. It's a play about characters brushing up against forces beyond their understanding: not just mortals at the mercy of fairies, but fairies themselves at the mercy of pure magic. All these fantastical twists come to represent a far less supernatural—far more common—encounter with the great, bewildering, primal, inscrutable force of love itself.

Love finds us, seduces us, disrupts us, controls us. It transforms us, and then it abandons us. The play takes these tropes and plants them like trees in the middle of an enchanted forest, makes them literal. Helena loves Demetrius, who loves Hermia, who loves Lysander, who loves Hermia back but doesn't have her father's permission to marry her. The would-be lovers flee Athens for the woods, where they get lost and their love wires get even *more* crossed by the fairy queen and king, Titania and Oberon, who are quarreling because they both love the same changeling boy too much to share him.

Love puts us at odds, turns us around, puts us in flight. Oberon orders his fairy servant Puck to set the square of lovers straight with the juice of a magical flower called "love-in-idleness," but he ends up making Lysander fall in love with Helena and everything gets even more confused. Titania falls in love with a man who has the head of an ass. Love-in-idleness is a white blossom "now purple with love's wound." The beauty of love is also a wound, an opening in the skin that exposes the flesh.

You could say: love gets strange once the fairies get involved. But obviously love has been strange all along. Their magic and spells only make explicit what anyone who has fallen in love already knows: it's bewildering and senseless, embarrassing and thrilling, confusing and overpowering all at once—impossible to predict, comprehend, or explain. "I have had a dream past the wit of man to say what dream it was," as Bottom says. He's talking about waking up with the head of an ass, but it's a pretty succinct way to talk about love. Who hasn't reached for language to describe a beloved and come up fumbling—hopelessly inadequate: *He's so sweet . . . She's so funny . . .* Every banal term of endearment is like Tupperware trying to hold a lightning strike.

After Bottom laments that his dream is "past the wit of man" to express, he imagines a better man—his companion Peter Quince— expressing it: "I will get Peter Quince to write a ballad of this dream. It shall be called 'Bottom's Dream,' because it hath no bottom."

The dream with no bottom. The day with no sunset. The forest with no rules. The fairies with no scruples. The mortals with no clue. Hermia finds the love of Demetrius and Lysander has cooled, while Helena finds it suddenly forceful. But I always found myself forgetting which one was Hermia and which one was Helena, which one was Demetrius and which one was Lysander. Perhaps this is the point: all the passionate convictions of love are a bit arbitrary, when you get right down to it. Who can say why we love one person rather than another?

When the fairy queen finds herself loving a man with the head of an ass, the whole play shrugs its shoulders the way each of us probably has—at our own desire, or the desire of another: Who can say where lust will attach itself? The heart wants what the heart wants. Bottom finds his body transformed into a walking punch line, and even the fairies find themselves humbled. This play is interested in the kind of love that overpowers us, takes us over entirely. None of it is particularly sentimental or sanguine. It's all as terrifying as it is thrilling; as embarrassing as it is intoxicating; as humbling and ultimately—horribly—arbitrary as it is consuming. The play is a comedy, and it ends with a double marriage, but by the time we arrive at the stability of marriage it has already tossed us around so much we can't believe in marriage as being much besides the sudden quieting of the music in an endless game of musical chairs.

Midsummer gets something deeply right about love—that it is intoxicating not *despite* being turbulent and overwhelming, as if these were opposing weights on a scale, but *because* it is turbulent and overwhelming; that some part of us *wants* to feel overwhelmed by emotion, and by destiny; that we want to put ourselves at the mercy of forces we can't quite understand. This hurling of ourselves is part of the appeal of magic, and ritual, and divinity, and love. We seek the gods that make us feel small: whether it's the burning bush of an Old Testament God, a stern old man in the sky, the pure brute force of an ocean tide, a lover's hand on the neck during sex. We devise rituals that let us summon and sculpt unmanageable forces. We court the limits of our own agency. We find the edges of what we understand and end up falling asleep on that strange border— waking up to find the world transformed, ourselves unrecognizable.

A *Midsummer Night's Dream* begins in the court, but its soul belongs to the forest. The court is ruled by law and order, but the forest is the realm of mayhem and enchantment, glorious and terrifying chaos. The court is where a father tells his daughter which man she is allowed to love, tells her she is "a form in wax" and should be pliable to his wishes—that she should submit her desires to the molds of custom. The forest is where she goes to elope with her lover. "If thou lovest me," Lysander pleads, "then / Steal forth thy father's house tomorrow night; / And in the wood, a league without the town, / . . . There will I stay for thee." The woods will launch them "to that place the sharp Athenian law / Cannot pursue." The woods are where the actors "may rehearse most obscenely and courageously," where art can get weird and bold and disturbing, where fantasy can veer toward the dangerous, where fathers don't get to say who gets to be loved; only fairies and flowers and fickleness get to do that. The psychic geography of the play acknowledges those margins lurking at the edge of any map: *Here be monsters. Here be fairies. Here be feelings we cannot fully master.* The world is marked by these places where the air shimmers with the spectral presence of hidden forces— places where things go awry or astray, where they are overturned or remade or reborn.

I've known a few of these places myself, where the boundary between the mundane and the magical grows thin; where everything feels holy and dangerous. These are places that make my molecules shiver, beds where it seems I could wake up with the head of a beast, or in love with one. Like the Wyoming hillside called the Thousand Acre, flecked with dry shrub brush and cattle bones, where I stood under a full moon and asked the night sky to save me from vanity; where the world felt rippling and opulent and I knew it was nothing I could make demands of—I could only squeeze my eyes closed and beg. Or the sweaty humidity of an underground bathhouse in the East Village, where I sat in a room as hot as a furnace until my body couldn't stand it anymore, then dumped wooden buckets of ice water over my baking skin until it steamed. Or the rickety old house teetering on a steep hill above a post office, where I stayed with a friend for a few weeks one summer, where we spent our hours writing, silently, furiously, lost to our worlds—and spent the evenings sitting in the shadow of a massive piece of brain coral while a lantern spackled the walls with lacy light, and read each other what we'd written. We listened hard. Those night hours, in that rickety house, made the air quiver and shiver, too, because we were wild for our art, desperate to get lost in it, to dream it and wake up to it. My writing felt like a lover.

It's no coincidence that the midsummer forest is midwife to love and art and magic all at once. Sometimes I suspect these are just three words we use to describe the same sensation—a wildness inside us that makes it difficult to sit still, that looks for trapdoors to burst from: stories and plays and kissing and fucking and painting and spell-casting and hydromancy and bonfires and rituals and song. Whenever we arrive in the forest, or the rickety house, or the thousand acres full of bones, the trapdoor flies open, and suddenly we are falling into the dream without a bottom.

✳

Marcel Dzama's drawings of the bottomless dream are full of palm fronds and low moons over turquoise waters; full of cigarettes swirling smoke into the night; full of stripes and polka dots and bathrobes and fairies and revelry and danger. Palm fronds melt like plastic over flame. Sex hangs like humidity in the air. The rocks have eyes. The trees have impish faces and drooping noses, with branches like clutching fingers full of malice and desire. Puck stands on his goat legs, playing his flute to the restless sea. The moon's reflection in the water seems to gaze up at the sky itself the way an adoring dog might stare at its master. A woman touches the bald head of the pale moon as if he were her lover. Perhaps he is. Perhaps he wants to be. It's so tender and perplexing and painful, the strange circuitry of desire: how we are followed by creatures that can't quit us; how we can't quit what we can't help loving. In the world of these drawings, you could fall in love with the moon, get pregnant from his glow, give birth to something made of light. In this world, your cigarette smoke might come alive, become a sprite, cast spells on you. In this world, the soil bubbles and boils. All the colors are bleeding: the wash of watercolor, the grassy streaks of chartreuse and mandarin and scarlet. The landscape brims with the intensity of consciousness: the peril and enchantment of being alive, having a body, falling in love, feeling subject—always, always—to forces larger than you could possibly understand.

The world of these drawings is caught somewhere between enchanted jungle and speakeasy. And what is a speakeasy if not an enchanted jungle, anyway—a space where someone could live beyond the rules for an evening, could become someone other than herself? Imagine Titania at the Cotton Club, with a low V in her polka-dot dress and a dark mask on her face, a cigarette dangling from her mouth. Her lipstick looks like dried blood. Her collarbones are sharp enough to cast shadows. She's got a wary look in her eyes like she's already slept with half the guys in the room and can't be bothered with the rest. The smoke from her cigarette seems almost sentient all around her, creating shapes that become clouds, that could become the bodies of fairies, flying restless through the night.

These drawings live somewhere between dream and nightmare. They refuse the distinction. They hold the uneasy emotional simultaneities of the play itself: intertwining enchantment and violence, freedom and danger, pleasure and pain. The drawings let all these things sit side by side, dance side by side, fuck and frolic side by side; they make a lie of any vision of the world that cannot hold them all. The faces of the fairies are full of mischief, malice, and exuberance all at once, bringing out what's sinister and frightening—not just blissful—about love and its insanities. In these drawings, magic doesn't simply grant your wishes. It deforms you. Freedom doesn't simply liberate you. It terrifies you. Transformation doesn't simply redeem you. It pains you. But maybe it also brings you to life. Bodies get caught in purgatories. Mid-metamorphosis, Bottom looks like a monster—both his human face and his ass head are visible, one shifting into the other. Transformation can leave you adrift in your own skin, without a body you can fathom. Under a fat-cheeked, inscrutable moon, a woman lounges in her polka-dot robe, and holds her cigarette at her crotch, where it looks almost like a thin penis pointed up at the sky, smoke streaming in an arc into the night. This is queer, too: the vixen coming. Her eyes look scared. She doesn't know what she is, what she's capable of, who or what she might impregnate.

In one drawing, Titania stands in a red dress with ragged white polka dots—their edges are messy, streaking down her silk—with palm trees drooping above her, tinged with banana yellow as if the vegetation were backlit by some strange light. Red blossoms lie at her feet like bursts of flame. A skull sits on the ground beside her— a reminder, amid all the lushness, that death still lurks in the rustling grass. All the magic in the world can't banish mortality. All the intoxication in the world can't make it go away. Titania holds two theater masks: tragedy in one hand, comedy in the other. So much of life is spent in this state of holding both at once, perched between. We never know whether to play our lives as suffering or farce. We are all standing in the humid heat, skulls at our ankles, trying to let life hold both.

In another drawing, Titania and Bottom look like a posh couple on vacation—in matching blue-and-white sundress and suit, her white-rimmed sunglasses and his bright eyes inside his ass's head, his gaze startled. He can't make sense of what he's become. In another drawing, they are dancing in a lush field flecked with brushstrokes of lime green and cinnabar, as though flames were licking at their bare feet in the grass, as though—perhaps—the grass has been made of flames all along. Bottom has the head of an ass and the silken shirt of a disco dancer, blue with white swirls that look lifted from the world around him—twisting clouds, or curls of cigarette smoke. His bare legs are pale and tender, his donkey head too heavy for his body. But he doesn't care. He's lost to the dance. Above his perked ears, two fairies soar like meteorites, trailing sparks across the cobalt sky. They've got pointy ears and wolfish grins and hair flying back from the speed of their flight.

After Bottom returns to his human form, his discarded donkey head lies like a carcass on the ground, tongue lolling. He's no longer dancing at the club, lounging like a baller with his fairy queen lover. The bottomless dream has found its bottom. Waking up is liberation for some, and for others it's just the return of the same old claustrophobia of ordinary life. Even restoration carries mourning. The natural order returns and flips on all the lights in the bar. It's closing time.

Once upon a time, I stood under a full moon in Wyoming and held an open purse to the sky. Once upon a time, my friend and I cast a love spell by throwing two loaves of bread into the Gowanus Canal. Once upon a time, I stood in the middle of the Gobi Desert and sent a flaming paper lantern upward into the night. Once upon a time, I sat with my mother on the grass of a convent in Burbank and we wrote our wishes on paper slips and burned them to ash.

That day on the convent grass, I had another slip of paper in my pocket: a prescription for antidepressants, from the shrink I'd just seen. He was an imposing man—tall and straight-backed, just this side of stern, with a single chair for me in the center of his office, as if I wcrc gctting intcrrogated. He got straight to the point. "Do you ever feel like you're seeing the world through shit-colored glasses?" he asked me, and the answer was not *yes*, but *always*. One thing I wrote on a slip of burning paper was: *I want to feel awe again.* Ritual and a prescription for Lamictal were two different ways to have a conversation with my own despair.

Ritual offers relief from our insides. It gives concrete vessels to our desires. It lets you want something with your hands and your body and your mouth, rather than just your mind. Its sympathetic magic takes interior longing—endless, impossible to grasp—and makes it something external and tangible: a loaf of bread turning soggy in the water; a paper lantern carried toward the moonstruck clouds. Ritual stems from the fantasy of making your pleas heard, of having some influence over all the things beyond influence. Ritual courts the parts of the universe we can't understand and beckons these mysterious registers closer. It believes that if you swim through the drain in the deep end of the pool, you'll reach the actual ocean.

That full moon in Wyoming was an October moon—also called the Hunter's Moon, the Dying Grass Moon, the Blood Moon. On a grassy field beneath a hillside littered with cattle bones, I stood in a circle with three other women, holding open our empty purses, and a man holding his empty wallet. We were all asking for something. We were supposed to say our desires aloud, so the others could echo them. Then the moon would fill our empty bags. I tried to be a good girl by asking for something that seemed spiritually enlightened, about not becoming obsessed with professional success. When of course I wanted everything: the best-seller lists, the prizes, the adoration of the masses. A love affair that would last for the rest of my life. Maybe a lake house. But instead I asked for the curbing of my own desires. The man who went next asked for a motorcycle. It clicked then: you can say what you please, but the heart wants what it wants. No point in pretending; the universe can see right through you.

It was Valentine's Day when my friend and I tossed our bread loaves into the oil-slicked Gowanus—maybe olive and sourdough? Who can remember what they were studded with, as they sank into the green shallows—and we were single, and we were tired of *thinking* about how we felt about being single, tired of *thinking* about all our broken loves, tired of *thinking*, period. We wanted to do something. We were tired of dissecting our insides until they bled the same shopworn truths we'd been coaxing from them for years—insights that didn't do much to dissolve our aloneness. My friend was a therapist, and I was a writer. We were professional insight-havers. We'd been betrayed too many times by the delusion that understanding a problem made it go away. Introspection always makes you feel like something is changing while you're doing it, but then it is done, and there you are—alone with yourself again. We were tired of introspection. We'd reached its limits, and on the far side of that border, we found ritual. In recovery, they said, *Sometimes the solution has nothing to do with the problem*, an idea I dismissed until I decided I probably needed to structure my entire life around it. Maybe ritual was one way of doing this. The solution to the problem of love might be a loaf of bread. It might be "a little western flower / . . . milk-white, now purple with love's wound." It might be an herb on the eyelids. It might be a paper lantern headed up toward a balsamic moon over Gobi dunes.

Five years later, my friend and I were both married with baby girls. So maybe the ritual worked. Two years after that, on Valentine's Day, I was dropping off my toddler with the sitter so I could sign my divorce papers. So maybe the ritual didn't work at all. Or maybe that's the deal with magic: It works on us, not for us. It never works according to our plans. Ritual and magic aren't forms of godly agency we claim; they are ways we brush up against the mystery of what we can't control. We holler our dreams at the big open sky. We empty our pockets and say, *Fill us up*. But we aren't ever in control, not really. We never know who will be standing there when our potion-dusted eyelids blink open.

The promise of ritual is transformation, which for me, at least, was once the siren call of booze: the instant liquid rearrangement of my interior. Frosted beer bottles and fireflies on humid nights. The simple promise that I could feel a different way than how I felt, almost immediately, that at the bottom of the bottle I could find a secret passageway out of myself.

The fantasy of booze is like the fantasy of ritual because both promise that something tangible—the dance, the offering, the bonfire, the glass, the sweet or the bitter or the bubbling—might change what feels immovable: that the burnt offering might conjure rain, or turn barrenness to fertility; that the amber syrup of whiskey might trick hurt into flight, or turn fear to recklessness. In the lusty, hallucinated washes of Dzama's drawings, I see the sparkling promise of intoxication, and also its grittier underbelly, the hard truth beneath the promise: the donkey's head lolling on the grass, unmoored and grotesque.

Ultimately, drinking was less about the cold slide of a perfect martini on a crisp night and more about a tongue furred with cheap Shiraz, tannin-tinted teeth, and a sloshing puddle in my belly, trapped inside the same sulk or shame. By the end, drinking felt less like enchantment and more like a fickle lover's bait and switch. Lysander loves Hermia until he doesn't. Booze worked until it stopped. Then it was just me and whatever feeling I was trying to get away from, only it was 2 AM and I was drunk and trying to remember where my car was parked and if I could squint hard enough against the blurry traffic lights to drive it home.

When I eventually got sober, I surrendered the dream of booze and replaced its fantasies of instant relief with a homelier set of promises—clarity, presence, open nerve endings—and a sturdier set of rituals: holding hands in church basements, setting up folding chairs, pouring coffee into Styrofoam cups, voices chanting in unison. These meetings were subterranean—marked by yellow basement windows glowing against cold nights, like signal flares. These meetings tasted like supermarket cookies and watery dark roast. They were how we got our knees with our voices: *The serenity to accept the things I cannot change; the courage to change the things I can.* They were a way of pleading for another version of what we'd wanted from booze: *Help us feel a different way than how we feel.*

I'd spent most of my life cultivating self-awareness and willpower, but in those rooms, I turned away from these old familiar gods. I submitted myself to technologies of surrender. Analyzing myself hadn't ever made me feel capable of constant sobriety, but maybe holding an old man's papery hand could—as we both begged for something we could not name, from forces we could not understand.

In those meetings, we read from big blue books that had been handled by hundreds of strangers in order to conjure something more expansive than the sum of our bodies. It was a formless creature made of our prayers and our despair and our hope.

A friend of mine got sober on the midwinter solstice. She said she heard *One day at a time* and decided she might as well get sober on the shortest day of the year. When I heard that, I thought, *The days are long. But the nights are even longer.*

Midwinter is the inverse of midsummer: it's bleak and depleted, but it's soaked with hope like a sponge. It's a hope based on faith and muscle memory more than on visible proof. You don't yet have the visual evidence of spring: the crops, the wildflowers, the green buds on the trees. You have just a few more minutes of daylight each morning and evening. You have to trust the change, because you can't yet see it in the trees. You have to feel it in your bones.

On the shortest day of the year, Russian villagers used to pour molten lead into freezing water as prophecy; the flowing metal hardened into shapes that were interpreted as predictions of the coming year. In ancient British folklore, the winter solstice marks the end of the waning-day reign of the Holly King, as he is defeated by his brother the Oak King, who brings the year back to summer. It's midwinter that marks the triumph of the summer brother. In this way, the shortest day of the year is also the one most fully turned toward light.

One Christmas, I found myself in an old cathedral in chilly Exeter while the day darkened—fully, early—just outside the stained-glass windows. My two-year-old daughter sat in my lap, sucking two fingers, as the choir sang "In the Bleak Midwinter." We were sitting on the cold stone floor of the cathedral because she'd gotten restless in the pews. It was a year into my separation, a year since I'd left my marriage. My nephew pressed against my side, whispering about the cathedral built of Legos just behind us. The voices of the choir surged and ached against the vaulted stone ceilings: *In the bleak midwinter, frosty wind made moan, | Earth stood hard as iron, water like a stone; |*

Snow had fallen, snow on snow, snow on snow . . . In that moment—on that cold stone floor, with the warm body of my daughter in my lap, and the warm body of my nephew leaning against my side, his silk hair falling on my arm—it seemed clear that hope was less about knowing what change would come and more about believing in the simple fact of change itself.

A month after that day in the cathedral, six friends gathered around my coffee table and we poured hot candle wax into a large salad bowl filled with ice water. It was our own version of pouring molten lead as prophecy. It was a frigid January night, a month before I signed divorce papers. My life felt chilly and molten at once—exposed to the elements, its shape undetermined. I knew that things were changing—that leaving my marriage had made it possible for them to change—but I didn't yet have any proof of what my life would become. When it was my turn to pour the wax into the water, the hardened shape I pulled out—pinched gently between my index finger and my thumb, dripping—looked like a sea cave, waxen tentacles forming an O like a mouth. What I really wanted was not another intoxicating love affair but a cave of my own, where I could make art, eat as much instant ramen as I wanted, and raise my daughter. It had nothing to do with love. It was about creation.

That winter of molten wax, I was living somewhere past the edges of the marriage plot. I'd fled the palace for the woods. Kneeling at the ice water—like Puck plucking love-in-idleness, like a supplicant taking the wafer of holy flesh—I was desperate to brush up against forces larger than I could understand. I was hungry for prophecy because the script of my life had gone rogue. The god-author who was supposed to drop me at the doorstep of a wedding's tidy narrative resolution—like Hippolyta and Theseus, Hermia and Lysander, Helena and Demetrius—was nowhere to be found. Or rather, she'd already done her work, but then I'd crossed out the ending of her manuscript and started scribbling over it with nothing but question marks: ????????????

Perhaps they call marriage "tying the knot" not only because it links two lives, two bank accounts, two futures, but because it promises a certain coherence—the braiding of all your loose strings. It seems to promise that all the ragged threads of your history, all the indulgences and indiscretions and betrayals and red herrings, might be gracefully subsumed by a narrative trajectory with a clear destination.

And yet, there I was, all my loose threads dangling—begging a bowl of ice water to offer my future as a lump of hardened candle wax, begging for reassurance that each solstice held the other in its grip, like a stowaway hidden in the cargo decks of a ship. I was desperate to believe that just as the bliss of midsummer holds the prospect of its own dissolve, so does the loneliness of midwinter hold the fetal promise of company. Every binary is always collapsing on itself: love holds fear; loss holds freedom; intimacy holds loneliness. New love sometimes gets chilly with old ghosts, like sudden breezes from a window left open at night. Bottom's transformation holds wonder and terror at once, just as his restoration holds both mourning and relief. The woods are full of skulls and dancing. The moon wants to make you come and it also wants to haunt your dreams. If fever is a signal of the body working beyond our sight, then magic is a signal of the universe doing the same. In the face of these impenetrable mysteries, we stay impatient. We stay bewildered. We stay hungry.

A Midsummer Night's Dream

Characters in the play

Four lovers
  HERMIA
  LYSANDER
  HELENA
  DEMETRIUS

THESEUS, duke of Athens
HIPPOLYTA, queen of the Amazons
EGEUS, father to Hermia
PHILOSTRATE, master of the revels to Theseus
NICK BOTTOM, a weaver
PETER QUINCE, a carpenter
FRANCIS FLUTE, a bellows-mender
TOM SNOUT, a tinker
SNUG, a joiner
ROBIN STARVELING, a tailor
OBERON, king of the Fairies
TITANIA, queen of the Fairies
PUCK, or Robin Goodfellow

Fairies attending upon Titania
  PEASEBLOSSOM
  COBWEB
  MOTE
  MUSTARDSEED

LORDS AND ATTENDANTS ON THESEUS AND HIPPOLYTA
OTHER FAIRIES IN THE TRAINS OF TITANIA AND OBERON

Act 1.

Scene 1.
Athens. The palace of Theseus

[*Enter Theseus, Hippolyta, Philostrate, and Attendants.*]

THESEUS   Now, fair Hippolyta, our nuptial hour
Draws on apace. Four happy days bring in
Another moon; but, O, methinks, how slow
This old moon wanes! She lingers* my desires,   *delays*
5   Like to a stepdame or a dowager
Long withering out* a young man's revenue.*   *diminishing | money*

HIPPOLYTA   Four days will quickly steep themselves in night;
Four nights will quickly dream away the time;
And then the moon, like to a silver bow
10   New-bent in heaven, shall behold the night
Of our solemnities.

THESEUS   Go, Philostrate,
Stir up the Athenian youth to merriments;
Awake the pert* and nimble spirit of mirth;   *lively*
15   Turn melancholy forth to funerals;
The pale companion* is not for our pomp.   *(contemptuous) fellow*
[*Philostrate exits.*]
Hippolyta, I wooed thee with my sword,
And won thy love, doing thee injuries;
But I will wed thee in another key,
20   With pomp, with triumph,* and with reveling.   *public festivity*

[*Enter Egeus, Hermia, Lysander, and Demetrius.*]

EGEUS   Happy be Theseus, our renownèd duke!

THESEUS   Thanks, good Egeus. What's the news with thee?

A midsummer desire under moonlight

EGEUS   Full of vexation come I, with complaint
Against my child, my daughter Hermia.
25   Stand forth, Demetrius. My noble lord,
This man hath my consent to marry her.
Stand forth, Lysander. And, my gracious duke,
This man hath bewitched the bosom of my child.
Thou, thou, Lysander, thou hast given her rhymes,
30   And interchanged love tokens with my child.
Thou hast by moonlight at her window sung,
With feigning voice, verses of feigning love,
And stol'n the impression of her fantasy*   *her imagination
With bracelets of thy hair, rings, gauds,* conceits,*   *playthings / trinkets
35   Knacks,* trifles, nosegays, sweetmeats, messengers   *Knickknacks
Of strong prevailment in unhardened youth.
With cunning hast thou filched my daughter's heart,
Turned her obedience, which is due to me,
To stubborn harshness. And, my gracious duke,
40   Be it so she will not here before your Grace
Consent to marry with Demetrius,
I beg the ancient privilege of Athens:
As she is mine, I may dispose of her,
Which shall be either to this gentleman
45   Or to her death, according to our law
Immediately provided in that case.

THESEUS   What say you, Hermia? Be advised, fair maid.
To you your father should be as a god,
One that composed your beauties, yea, and one
50   To whom you are but as a form in wax
By him imprinted and within his power
To leave the figure or disfigure it.
Demetrius is a worthy gentleman.

HERMIA   So is Lysander.

55   THESEUS   In himself he is;
But in this kind, wanting your father's voice,*   *lacking your father's approval
The other must be held the worthier.

HERMIA   I would my father looked but with my eyes.

THESEUS   Rather your eyes must with his judgment look.

60 HERMIA   I do entreat your grace to pardon me.
I know not by what power I am made bold,
Nor how it may concern my modesty,
In such a presence here to plead my thoughts;
But I beseech your Grace that I may know
65 The worst that may befall me in this case,
If I refuse to wed Demetrius.

THESEUS   Either to die the death, or to abjure
Forever the society of men.
Therefore, fair Hermia, question your desires;
70 Know of your youth, examine well your blood,*   *passions
Whether, if you yield not to your father's choice,
You can endure the livery of a nun,
For aye* to be in shady cloister mewed,*   *Forever / caged
To live a barren sister all your life,
75 Chanting faint hymns to the cold fruitless moon.*   *Diana (goddess of chastity and the moon)
Thrice-blessèd they that master so their blood
To undergo such maiden pilgrimage;
But earthlier happy is the rose distilled,*   *made into perfume
Than that which, withering on the virgin thorn,
80 Grows, lives, and dies in single blessedness.

HERMIA   So will I grow, so live, so die, my lord,
Ere I will yield my virgin patent* up   *privilege
Unto his lordship, whose unwished yoke
My soul consents not to give sovereignty.

85 THESEUS   Take time to pause; and, by the next new moon—
The sealing day betwixt my love and me,
For everlasting bond of fellowship—
Upon that day either prepare to die
For disobedience to your father's will,
90 Or else to wed Demetrius, as he would,

2020

marcel Dzama

When rock becomes air

Or on Diana's altar to protest*   *vow*
For aye austerity and single life.

DEMETRIUS   Relent, sweet Hermia: and, Lysander, yield
Thy crazèd title* to my certain right.   *flawed claim*

95   LYSANDER   You have her father's love, Demetrius;
Let me have Hermia's: do you marry him.

EGEUS   Scornful Lysander! True, he hath my love,
And what is mine my love shall render him.
And she is mine, and all my right of her
100   I do estate unto* Demetrius.   *give to*

LYSANDER   I am, my lord, as well derived as he,
As well possessed;* my love is more than his;   *rich*
My fortunes every way as fairly ranked,
If not with vantage,* as Demetrius';   *even better*
105   And, which is more than all these boasts can be,
I am beloved of beauteous Hermia.
Why should not I then prosecute my right?
Demetrius, I'll avouch it to his head,
Made love to Nedar's daughter, Helena,
110   And won her soul; and she, sweet lady, dotes,
Devoutly dotes, dotes in idolatry,
Upon this spotted* and inconstant man.   *morally stained*

THESEUS   I must confess that I have heard so much,
And with Demetrius thought to have spoke thereof;
115   But, being overfull of self-affairs,
My mind did lose it. But, Demetrius, come;
And come, Egeus; you shall go with me,
I have some private schooling for you both.
For you, fair Hermia, look you arm yourself
120   To fit your fancies to your father's will;
Or else the law of Athens yields you up—
Which by no means we may extenuate—
To death, or to a vow of single life.

Come, my Hippolyta. What cheer, my love?
125 Demetrius and Egeus, go along.
I must employ you in some business
Against* our nuptial and confer with you   *In preparation for*
Of something nearly* that concerns yourselves.   *closely*

EGEUS   With duty and desire we follow you.

[*Exit all but Lysander and Hermia.*]

130 LYSANDER   How now, my love! Why is your cheek so pale?
How chance the roses there do fade so fast?

HERMIA   Belike* for want* of rain, which I could well   *Perhaps | lack*
Beteem* them from the tempest of my eyes.   *Bring*

LYSANDER   Ay me! For aught that I could ever read,
135 Could ever hear by tale or history,
The course of true love never did run smooth;
But, either it was different in blood—

HERMIA   O cross! Too high to be enthralled to low.

LYSANDER   Or else misgraffèd* in respect of years—   *mismatched*

140 HERMIA   O spite! Too old to be engaged to young.

LYSANDER   Or else it stood upon the choice of friends—

HERMIA   O hell! To choose love by another's eyes.

LYSANDER   Or, if there were a sympathy in choice,
War, death, or sickness did lay siege to it,
145 Making it momentany* as a sound,   *momentary*
Swift as a shadow, short as any dream;
Brief as the lightning in the collied* night,   *blackened*
That, in a spleen,* unfolds both heaven and earth,   *flash*
And ere a man hath power to say "Behold!"

150 The jaws of darkness do devour it up:
So quick bright things come to confusion.

HERMIA   If then true lovers have been ever crossed,
It stands as an edict in destiny:
Then let us teach our trial* patience,   *teach ourselves*
155 Because it is a customary cross,
As due to love as thoughts and dreams and sighs,
Wishes and tears, poor fancy's* followers.   *love's*

LYSANDER   A good persuasion. Therefore, hear me, Hermia.
I have a widow aunt, a dowager
160 Of great revenue, and she hath no child.
From Athens is her house remote seven leagues;
And she respects me as her only son.
There, gentle Hermia, may I marry thee;
And to that place the sharp Athenian law
165 Cannot pursue us. If thou lovest me, then
Steal forth thy father's house tomorrow night;
And in the wood, a league without the town,
Where I did meet thee once with Helena,
To do observance to a morn of May,
170 There will I stay for thee.

HERMIA   My good Lysander!
I swear to thee, by Cupid's strongest bow,
By his best arrow with the golden head,
By the simplicity of Venus' doves,
175 By that which knitteth souls and prospers loves,
And by that fire which burned the Carthage queen,
When the false Trojan under sail was seen,
By all the vows that ever men have broke,
In number more than ever women spoke,
180 In that same place thou hast appointed me,
Tomorrow truly will I meet with thee.

LYSANDER   Keep promise, love. Look, here comes Helena.

[Enter Helena.]

HERMIA   God speed fair Helena! Whither away?

HELENA   Call you me fair? That fair again unsay.
185 Demetrius loves your fair.* O happy fair!   *beauty*
     Your eyes are lodestars;* and your tongue's sweet air*   *guiding stars | music*
     More tunable than lark to shepherd's ear,
     When wheat is green, when hawthorn buds appear.
     Sickness is catching. O, were favor* so,   *looks*
190 Yours would I catch, fair Hermia, ere I go;
     My ear should catch your voice, my eye your eye,
     My tongue should catch your tongue's sweet melody.
     Were the world mine, Demetrius being bated,*   *excepted*
     The rest I'd give to be to you translated.*   *transformed*
195 O, teach me how you look, and with what art
     You sway the motion of Demetrius' heart!

HERMIA   I frown upon him, yet he loves me still.

HELENA   O that your frowns would teach my smiles such skill!

HERMIA   I give him curses, yet he gives me love.

200 HELENA   O that my prayers could such affection move!

HERMIA   The more I hate, the more he follows me.

HELENA   The more I love, the more he hateth me.

HERMIA   His folly, Helena, is no fault of mine.

HELENA   None, but your beauty: would that fault were mine!

205 HERMIA   Take comfort: he no more shall see my face;
     Lysander and myself will fly this place.
     Before the time I did Lysander see,
     Seemed Athens as a paradise to me:

A song that rouses passions

O, then, what graces in my love do dwell,
210 That he hath turned a heaven unto a hell!

LYSANDER   Helen, to you our minds we will unfold:
Tomorrow night, when Phoebe* doth behold   *the moon (Diana)*
Her silver visage in the wat'ry glass,*   *pond*
Decking with liquid pearl the bladed grass,
215 A time that lovers' flights doth still* conceal,   *always*
Through Athens' gates have we devised to steal.

HERMIA   And in the wood, where often you and I
Upon faint primrose beds were wont to lie,
Emptying our bosoms of their counsel sweet,
220 There my Lysander and myself shall meet;
And thence from Athens turn away our eyes,
To seek new friends and stranger companies.
Farewell, sweet playfellow. Pray thou for us;
And good luck grant thee thy Demetrius!
225 Keep word, Lysander. We must starve our sight
From lovers' food till morrow deep midnight.

LYSANDER   I will, my Hermia. [*Hermia exits.*]
                                        Helena, adieu.
As you on him, Demetrius dote on you! [*He exits.*]

230 HELENA   How happy some o'er other some* can be!   *in comparison with others*
Through Athens I am thought as fair as she.
But what of that? Demetrius thinks not so;
He will not know what all but he do know.
And as he errs, doting on Hermia's eyes,
235 So I, admiring of his qualities.
Things base and vile, holding no quantity,*   *having no proportion (unattractive)*
Love can transpose to form and dignity.
Love looks not with the eyes, but with the mind;
And therefore is winged Cupid painted blind.
240 Nor hath Love's mind of any judgment taste;
Wings, and no eyes, figure* unheedy haste: *represent*
And therefore is Love said to be a child,

Because in choice he is so oft beguiled.
As waggish boys in game themselves forswear,
245   So the boy Love is perjured everywhere.
For ere Demetrius looked on Hermia's eyne,*   *eyes*
He hailed down oaths that he was only mine;
And when this hail some heat from Hermia felt,
So he dissolved, and show'rs of oaths did melt.
250   I will go tell him of fair Hermia's flight.
Then to the wood will he tomorrow night
Pursue her; and for this intelligence*   *news*
If I have thanks, it is a dear expense:
But herein mean I to enrich my pain,
255   To have his sight thither and back again.

[*She exits.*]

Scene 2.
Athens. Quince's house

[Enter Quince, Snug, Bottom, Flute, Snout, and Starveling.]

QUINCE   Is all our company here?

BOTTOM   You were best to call them generally,* man by man,   *("individually" meant)*
according to the scrip.

QUINCE   Here is the scroll of every man's name, which is thought
5   fit, through all Athens, to play in our interlude before the duke
and the duchess, on his wedding day at night.

BOTTOM   First, good Peter Quince, say what the play treats on,
then read the names of the actors, and so grow to a point.

QUINCE   Marry, our play is "The most lamentable comedy, and
10   most cruel death of Pyramus and Thisby."

BOTTOM   A very good piece of work, I assure you, and a merry.
Now, good Peter Quince, call forth your actors by the scroll.
Masters, spread yourselves.

QUINCE   Answer as I call you. Nick Bottom, the weaver.

15   BOTTOM   Ready. Name what part I am for, and proceed.

QUINCE   You, Nick Bottom, are set down for Pyramus.

BOTTOM   What is Pyramus? A lover, or a tyrant?

QUINCE   A lover that kills himself most gallant for love.

BOTTOM   That will ask some tears in the true performing of it: if I do it,
20 let the audience look to their eyes; I will move storms, I will condole*   *lament*
in some measure. To the rest: yet my chief humor* is for a tyrant.   *disposition*
I could play Ercles* rarely, or a part to tear a cat* in, to make all split.   *Hercules | rant*
      The raging rocks
      And shivering shocks
25   Shall break the locks
      Of prison gates;
      And Phibbus' car*   *(chariot of the sun god, Phoebus, meant)*
      Shall shine from far
      And make and mar
30   The foolish Fates.
This was lofty! Now name the rest of the players. This is Ercles' vein,
a tyrant's vein. A lover is more condoling.

QUINCE   Francis Flute, the bellows-mender.

FLUTE   Here, Peter Quince.

35 QUINCE   Flute, you must take Thisby on you.

FLUTE   What is Thisby? A wand'ring knight?

QUINCE   It is the lady that Pyramus must love.

FLUTE   Nay, faith, let not me play a woman. I have a beard coming.

QUINCE   That's all one.* You shall play it in a mask, and   *It makes no difference*
40 you may speak as small as you will.

BOTTOM   An* I may hide my face, let me play Thisby too, I'll speak in   *If*
a monstrous little voice. "Thisne, Thisne!" "Ah, Pyramus, my lover dear!
Thy Thisby dear, and lady dear!"

QUINCE   No, no; you must play Pyramus: and, Flute, you Thisby.

45 BOTTOM   Well, proceed.

QUINCE   Robin Starveling, the tailor.

STARVELING   Here, Peter Quince.

QUINCE   Robin Starveling, you must play Thisby's mother. Tom Snout, the tinker.

50   SNOUT   Here, Peter Quince.

QUINCE   You, Pyramus' father: myself, Thisby's father: Snug, the joiner; you, the lion's part: and I hope here is a play fitted.

SNUG   Have you the lion's part written? Pray you, if it be, give it me, for I am slow of study.

55   QUINCE   You may do it extempore, for it is nothing but roaring.

BOTTOM   Let me play the lion too. I will roar, that I will do any man's heart good to hear me. I will roar, that I will make the duke say, "Let him roar again, let him roar again."

QUINCE   An you should do it too terribly, you would fright the
60   duchess and the ladies, that they would shriek; and that were enough to hang us all.

ALL   That would hang us, every mother's son.

BOTTOM   I grant you, friends, if you should fright the ladies out of their wits, they would have no more discretion but to hang us:
65   but I will aggravate* my voice so that I will roar you as gently as   *("moderate" meant)
any sucking dove; I will roar you an 'twere* any nightingale.   *as if it were

QUINCE   You can play no part but Pyramus; for Pyramus is a sweet-faced man; a proper* man, as one shall see in a summer's day; a most   *handsome
lovely gentlemanlike man: therefore you must needs play Pyramus.

70   BOTTOM   Well, I will undertake it. What beard were I best to play it in?

QUINCE   Why, what you will.

BOTTOM   I will discharge it in either your straw-color beard,
your orange-tawny beard, your purple-in-grain beard, or your French-
crown-color beard, your perfit* yellow.   *perfect*

75 QUINCE   Some of your French crowns have no hair at all, and then
you will play barefaced.* But, masters, here are your parts; and I am   *brazen*
to entreat you, request you, and desire you, to con* them by tomorrow   *study*
night, and meet me in the palace wood, a mile without the town,
by moonlight. There will we rehearse, for if we meet in the city,
80 we shall be dogged with company, and our devices* known. In the   *plans*
meantime I will draw a bill of properties, such as our play wants.
I pray you, fail me not.

BOTTOM   We will meet; and there we may rehearse most obscenely*   *("seemly" meant)*
and courageously. Take pains; be perfit: adieu.

85 QUINCE   At the Duke's Oak we meet.

BOTTOM   Enough; hold or cut bowstrings.

[*They exit.*]

Act 2.

Scene 1.
A wood near Athens

[*Enter, from opposite sides, a Fairy and Puck.*]

PUCK How now, spirit! Whither wander you?

FAIRY Over hill, over dale,
    Thorough bush, thorough brier,
    Over park, over pale,*   *enclosed land*
5   Thorough flood, thorough fire,
    I do wander everywhere,
    Swifter than the moon's sphere;
    And I serve the Fairy Queen,
    To dew her orbs upon the green.
10   The cowslips tall her pensioners* be: *bodyguards*
    In their gold coats spots you see;
    Those be rubies, fairy favors,*   *gifts*
    In those freckles live their savors.*   *perfumes*
I must go seek some dewdrops here
15 And hang a pearl in every cowslip's ear.
Farewell, thou lob* of spirits; I'll be gone: *oaf*
Our queen and all our elves come here anon.*   *soon*

PUCK The king doth keep his revels here tonight.
Take heed the queen come not within his sight.
20 For Oberon is passing fell and wrath,*   *fierce and angry*
Because that she as her attendant hath
A lovely boy, stolen from an Indian king;
She never had so sweet a changeling.
And jealous Oberon would have the child
25 Knight of his train, to trace the forests wild.
But she perforce withholds the lovèd boy,
Crowns him with flowers and makes him all her joy.

And now they never meet in grove or green,
By fountain clear, or spangled starlight sheen,
30 But they do square,* that all their elves for fear   *quarrel*
Creep into acorn cups and hide them there.

FAIRY   Either I mistake your shape and making quite,
Or else you are that shrewd and knavish sprite
Called Robin Goodfellow. Are not you he
35 That frights the maidens of the villagery;*   *villagers*
Skim milk, and sometimes labor in the quern*   *mill for grinding grain*
And bootless* make the breathless housewife churn;   *fruitlessly*
And sometime make the drink to bear no barm;*   *froth on beer*
Mislead night-wanderers, laughing at their harm?
40 Those that Hobgoblin call you and sweet Puck,
You do their work, and they shall have good luck.
Are not you he?

PUCK   Thou speakest aright;
I am that merry wanderer of the night.
45 I jest to Oberon and make him smile
When I a fat and bean-fed horse beguile,
Neighing in likeness of a filly foal:
And sometime lurk I in a gossip's bowl,
In very likeness of a roasted crab,*   *crab apple*
50 And when she drinks, against her lips I bob
And on her withered dewlap* pour the ale.   *fold of skin on the throat*
The wisest aunt, telling the saddest tale,
Sometime for three-foot stool mistaketh me;
Then slip I from her bum, down topples she,
55 And "tailor" cries, and falls into a cough;
And then the whole quire* hold their hips and laugh,   *company, choir*
And waxen* in their mirth and neeze* and swear   *increase | sneeze*
A merrier hour was never wasted* there.   *passed*
But, room, fairy! Here comes Oberon.

60 FAIRY   And here my mistress. Would that he were gone!

[*Enter, from one side, Oberon, with his train; from the other, Titania, with hers.*]

2020   marcel DZAMA

The merrier hour was never wasted   45

marcel DzAMA

I must be thy lady

OBERON   Ill met by moonlight, proud Titania.

TITANIA   What, jealous Oberon! Fairies, skip hence:
I have forsworn his bed and company.

OBERON   Tarry, rash wanton. Am not I thy lord?

65 TITANIA   Then I must be thy lady: but I know
When thou hast stolen away from fairy land,
And in the shape of Corin* sat all day,   *traditional shepherd in pastoral poetry
Playing on pipes of corn and versing love
To amorous Phillida.* Why art thou here,   *traditional shepherdess in pastoral poetry
70 Come from the farthest steep of India?
But that, forsooth,* the bouncing Amazon,   *in truth
Your buskined* mistress and your warrior love,   *wearing boots
To Theseus must be wedded, and you come
To give their bed joy and prosperity.

75 OBERON   How canst thou thus for shame, Titania,
Glance at my credit with Hippolyta,
Knowing I know thy love to Theseus?
Didst not thou lead him through the glimmering night
From Perigenia, whom he ravishèd?
80 And make him with fair Aegles break his faith,
With Ariadne and Antiopa?

TITANIA   These are the forgeries of jealousy:
And never, since the middle summer's spring,*   *beginning of midsummer
Met we on hill, in dale, forest, or mead,
85 By pavèd* fountain or by rushy brook,   *pebbly
Or in the beachèd margent* of the sea,   *shore
To dance our ringlets* to the whistling wind,   *circle dances
But with thy brawls thou hast disturbed our sport.
Therefore the winds, piping to us in vain,
90 As in revenge, have sucked up from the sea
Contagious fogs; which, falling in the land,
Hath every pelting* river made so proud   *insignificant
That they have overborne their continents.*   *banks

The ox hath therefore stretched his yoke in vain,

95 The plowman lost his sweat, and the green corn
Hath rotted ere his youth attained a beard;
The fold* stands empty in the drownèd field,   *pen*
And crows are fatted with the murrion flock;*   *flock dead of infectious disease*
The nine men's morris* is filled up with mud,   *space cut in the turf for a game*
100 And the quaint mazes in the wanton green,
For lack of tread, are undistinguishable.
The human mortals want* their winter here;   *lack*
No night is now with hymn or carol blest.
Therefore the moon, the governess of floods,
105 Pale in her anger, washes all the air,
That rheumatic diseases do abound.
And thorough this distemperature* we see   *bad weather*
The seasons alter: hoary-headed frosts
Fall in the fresh lap of the crimson rose,
110 And on old Hiems'* thin and icy crown   *the winter's*
An odorous chaplet* of sweet summer buds   *wreath*
Is, as in mockery, set. The spring, the summer,
The childing* autumn, angry winter, change   *fruitful*
Their wonted liveries,* and the mazèd* world,   *usual apparel / bewildered*
115 By their increase, now knows not which is which.
And this same progeny of evils comes
From our debate,* from our dissension;   *quarrel*
We are their parents and original.

OBERON   Do you amend it then; it lies in you:
120 Why should Titania cross her Oberon?
I do but beg a little changeling boy,
To be my henchman.*   *page*

TITANIA   Set your heart at rest:
The fairy land buys not the child of me.
125 His mother was a vot'ress* of my order,   *woman who has taken a vow*
And, in the spicèd Indian air, by night,
Full often hath she gossiped by my side,
And sat with me on Neptune's* yellow sands,   *god of the sea*
Marking th' embarkèd traders on the flood,

130 When we have laughed to see the sails conceive
And grow big-bellied with the wanton wind;
Which she, with pretty and with swimming gait
Following—her womb then rich with my young squire—
Would imitate, and sail upon the land,
135 To fetch me trifles, and return again,
As from a voyage, rich with merchandise.
But she, being mortal, of that boy did die;
And for her sake do I rear up her boy,
And for her sake I will not part with him.

140 OBERON   How long within this wood intend you stay?

TITANIA   Perchance till after Theseus' wedding day.
If you will patiently dance in our round*   *circle dance
And see our moonlight revels, go with us.
If not, shun me, and I will spare* your haunts.   *keep away from

145 OBERON   Give me that boy, and I will go with thee.

TITANIA   Not for thy fairy kingdom. Fairies, away!
We shall chide downright, if I longer stay. [*Titania exits with her train.*]

OBERON   Well, go thy way. Thou shalt not from this grove
Till I torment thee for this injury.
150 My gentle Puck, come hither. Thou rememb'rest
Since* once I sat upon a promontory,   *When
And heard a mermaid on a dolphin's back
Uttering such dulcet and harmonious breath
That the rude sea grew civil at her song
155 And certain stars shot madly from their spheres
To hear the sea-maid's music.

PUCK   I remember.

OBERON   That very time I saw, but thou couldst not,
Flying between the cold moon and the earth,
160 Cupid all armed. A certain aim he took

At a fair vestal* thronèd by the west,   *virgin*
And loosed his love-shaft smartly from his bow,
As it should pierce a hundred thousand hearts.
But I might* see young Cupid's fiery shaft   *could*
165 Quenched in the chaste beams of the wat'ry moon,
And the imperial vot'ress passèd on,
In maiden meditation, fancy-free.
Yet marked I where the bolt of Cupid fell.
It fell upon a little western flower,
170 Before milk-white, now purple with love's wound,
And maidens call it love-in-idleness.*   *pansy flower*
Fetch me that flower; the herb I showed thee once:
The juice of it on sleeping eyelids laid
Will make or* man or woman madly dote   *either*
175 Upon the next live creature that it sees.
Fetch me this herb, and be thou here again
Ere the leviathan can swim a league.

PUCK   I'll put a girdle round about the earth
In forty minutes. [*He exits.*]

180 OBERON   Having once this juice,
I'll watch Titania when she is asleep,
And drop the liquor of it in her eyes.
The next thing then she waking looks upon,
Be it on lion, bear, or wolf, or bull,
185 On meddling monkey, or on busy ape,
She shall pursue it with the soul of love.
And ere I take this charm from off her sight,
As I can take it with another herb,
I'll make her render up her page to me.
190 But who comes here? I am invisible,
And I will overhear their conference.

[*Enter Demetrius, Helena following him.*]

DEMETRIUS   I love thee not, therefore pursue me not.
Where is Lysander and fair Hermia?

2020   A MERMAID ON A DOLPHIN'S BACK UTTERING HARMONIOUS BREATH   MARCEL DZAMA

A mermaid on a dolphin's back, uttering harmonious breath   51

The one I'll slay, the other slayeth me.
195 Thou told'st me they were stol'n unto this wood;
And here am I, and wood* within this wood,   *insane
Because I cannot meet my Hermia.
Hence, get thee gone, and follow me no more.

HELENA   You draw me, you hard-hearted adamant;*   *magnet
200 But yet you draw not iron, for my heart
Is true as steel. Leave you your power to draw,
And I shall have no power to follow you.

DEMETRIUS   Do I entice you? Do I speak you fair?
Or, rather, do I not in plainest truth
205 Tell you I do not nor I cannot love you?

HELENA   And even for that do I love you the more.
I am your spaniel; and, Demetrius,
The more you beat me, I will fawn on you.
Use me but as your spaniel, spurn me, strike me,
210 Neglect me, lose me; only give me leave,
Unworthy as I am, to follow you.
What worser place can I beg in your love—
And yet a place of high respect with me—
Than to be usèd as you use your dog?

215 DEMETRIUS   Tempt not too much the hatred of my spirit,
For I am sick when I do look on thee.

HELENA   And I am sick when I look not on you.

DEMETRIUS   You do impeach* your modesty too much,   *discredit
To leave the city and commit yourself
220 Into the hands of one that loves you not,
To trust the opportunity of night
And the ill counsel of a desert place
With the rich worth of your virginity.

HELENA   Your virtue is my privilege.* For that   *protection*
225 It is not night when I do see your face,
Therefore I think I am not in the night;
Nor doth this wood lack worlds of company,
For you in my respect* are all the world.   *opinion*
Then how can it be said I am alone,
230 When all the world is here to look on me?

DEMETRIUS   I'll run from thee and hide me in the brakes,*   *thickets*
And leave thee to the mercy of wild beasts.

HELENA   The wildest hath not such a heart as you.
Run when you will, the story shall be changed:
235 Apollo flies, and Daphne holds the chase;
The dove pursues the griffin; the mild hind*   *doe*
Makes speed to catch the tiger; bootless speed,
When cowardice pursues and valor flies.

DEMETRIUS   I will not stay* thy questions. Let me go,   *stay for*
240 Or, if thou follow me, do not believe
But I shall do thee mischief in the wood.

HELENA   Ay, in the temple, in the town, the field,
You do me mischief. Fie, Demetrius!
Your wrongs do set a scandal on my sex.
245 We cannot fight for love, as men may do.
We should be wooed and were not made to woo.
[*Demetrius exits.*]
I'll follow thee and make a heaven of hell,
To die upon the hand I love so well. [*She exits.*]

OBERON   Fare thee well, nymph: ere he do leave this grove,
250 Thou shalt fly him, and he shall seek thy love.
[*Enter Puck.*]
Hast thou the flower there? Welcome, wanderer.

PUCK   Ay, there it is.

2020   marcel Dzama

I know a flower of evil   54

OBERON   I pray thee, give it me.
I know a bank where the wild thyme blows,
255 Where oxlips and the nodding violet grows,
Quite overcanopied with luscious woodbine,
With sweet musk-roses and with eglantine.
There sleeps Titania sometime of the night,
Lulled in these flowers with dances and delight;
260 And there the snake throws* her enameled skin,   *casts off*
Weed* wide enough to wrap a fairy in.   *Garment*
And with the juice of this I'll streak her eyes,
And make her full of hateful fantasies.
Take thou some of it, and seek through this grove.
265 A sweet Athenian lady is in love
With a disdainful youth. Anoint his eyes;
But do it when the next thing he espies
May be the lady. Thou shalt know the man
By the Athenian garments he hath on.
270 Effect it with some care, that he may prove
More fond on her than she upon her love:
And look thou meet me ere the first cock crow.

PUCK   Fear not, my lord, your servant shall do so.

[*They exit.*]

Scene 2.
Another part of the wood

[Enter Titania, with her train.]

TITANIA   Come, now a roundel* and a fairy song;   *circle dance*
Then, for the third part of a minute, hence;
Some to kill cankers in the musk-rose buds,
Some war with reremice* for their leathern wings   *bats*
5   To make my small elves coats, and some keep back
The clamorous owl that nightly hoots and wonders
At our quaint* spirits. Sing me now asleep.   *dainty*
Then to your offices and let me rest.

[The fairies sing.]

FIRST FAIRY   *You spotted snakes with double* tongue,*   *forked*
10   *Thorny hedgehogs, be not seen;*
Newts and blindworms, do no wrong,
Come not near our fairy queen.

CHORUS   *Philomel, with melody*
Sing in our sweet lullaby;
15   *Lulla, lulla, lullaby, lulla, lulla, lullaby:*
Never harm,
Nor spell nor charm,
Come our lovely lady nigh;
So, good night, with lullaby.

20   FIRST FAIRY   *Weaving spiders, come not here;*
Hence, you long-legged spinners, hence!
Beetles black, approach not near;
Worm nor snail, do no offense.

2020

marcel DZAMA

Sing me now asleep

CHORUS   *Philomel, with melody*
25 *Sing in our sweet lullaby;*
    Lulla, lulla, lullaby, lulla, lulla, lullaby:
    Never harm,
    Nor spell nor charm,
    Come our lovely lady nigh;
30 *So, good night, with lullaby.*

FAIRY   Hence, away! Now all is well.
One aloof stand sentinel. [*Fairies exit. Titania sleeps.*]

[*Enter Oberon and squeezes the flower on Titania's eyelids.*]

OBERON   What thou seest when thou dost wake,
        Do it for thy true love take;
35   Love and languish for his sake.
        Be it ounce,* or cat, or bear,   *lynx*
        Pard,* or boar with bristled hair,   *Leopard*
        In thy eye that shall appear
        When thou wak'st, it is thy dear.
40   Wake when some vile thing is near. [*He exits.*]

[*Enter Lysander and Hermia.*]

LYSANDER   Fair love, you faint with wand'ring in the wood;
And to speak troth,* I have forgot our way.   *truth*
We'll rest us, Hermia, if you think it good,
And tarry* for the comfort of the day.   *wait*

45 HERMIA   Be it so, Lysander. Find you out a bed;
For I upon this bank will rest my head.

LYSANDER   One turf shall serve as pillow for us both;
One heart, one bed, two bosoms, and one troth.*   *vow*

HERMIA   Nay, good Lysander. For my sake, my dear,
50 Lie further off yet, do not lie so near.

LYSANDER   O, take the sense, sweet, of my innocence!
Love takes the meaning in love's conference.
I mean, that my heart unto yours is knit,
So that but one heart we can make of it;
55   Two bosoms interchained with an oath;
So then two bosoms and a single troth.
Then by your side no bed-room me deny;
For lying so, Hermia, I do not lie.

HERMIA   Lysander riddles very prettily.
60   Now much beshrew* my manners and my pride,   *curse*
If Hermia meant to say Lysander lied.
But, gentle friend, for love and courtesy
Lie further off, in human modesty.
Such separation as may well be said
65   Becomes a virtuous bachelor and a maid,
So far be distant; and, good night, sweet friend.
Thy love ne'er alter till thy sweet life end!

LYSANDER   Amen, amen, to that fair prayer, say I,
And then end life when I end loyalty!
70   Here is my bed. Sleep give thee all his rest!

HERMIA   With half that wish the wisher's eyes be pressed! [*They sleep.*]

[*Enter Puck.*]

PUCK   Through the forest have I gone.
But Athenian found I none,
On whose eyes I might approve*   *test*
75   This flower's force in stirring love.
Night and silence.—Who is here?
Weeds* of Athens he doth wear: *Garments*
This is he, my master said,
Despisèd the Athenian maid;
80   And here the maiden, sleeping sound,
On the dank and dirty ground.
Pretty soul! She durst not lie

2020

marcel DZAMA

Asleep near the ocean

Near this lack-love, this kill-courtesy.
Churl,* upon thy eyes I throw   *Boorish person*
All the power this charm doth owe.*   *possess*

85

When thou wak'st, let love forbid
Sleep his seat on thy eyelid.
So awake when I am gone;
For I must now to Oberon. [*He exits.*]

[*Enter Demetrius and Helena, running.*]

90   HELENA   Stay, though thou kill me, sweet Demetrius.

DEMETRIUS   I charge thee, hence, and do not haunt me thus.

HELENA   O, wilt thou darkling* leave me? Do not so.   *in the dark*

DEMETRIUS   Stay, on thy peril. I alone will go. [*He exits.*]

HELENA   O, I am out of breath in this fond* chase!   *foolish; doting*
95   The more my prayer, the lesser is my grace.*   *favor*
Happy is Hermia, wheresoe'er she lies,
For she hath blessèd and attractive eyes.
How came her eyes so bright? Not with salt tears.
If so, my eyes are oftener washed than hers.
100   No, no, I am as ugly as a bear,
For beasts that meet me run away for fear.
Therefore no marvel though Demetrius
Do, as a monster, fly my presence thus.
What wicked and dissembling glass of mine
105   Made me compare with Hermia's sphery eyne?*   *starry eyes*
But who is here? Lysander! On the ground!
Dead? Or asleep? I see no blood, no wound.
Lysander if you live, good sir, awake.

LYSANDER   [*Awaking*] And run through fire I will for thy sweet sake.
110   Transparent* Helena! Nature shows art,   *Radiant*
That through thy bosom makes me see thy heart.
Where is Demetrius? O, how fit a word
Is that vile name to perish on my sword!

HELENA   Do not say so, Lysander, say not so.
115   What though he love your Hermia? Lord, what though?
Yet Hermia still loves you. Then be content.

LYSANDER   Content with Hermia! No; I do repent
The tedious minutes I with her have spent.
Not Hermia but Helena I love:
120   Who will not change a raven for a dove?
The will* of man is by his reason swayed;   *desire*
And reason says you are the worthier maid.
Things growing are not ripe until their season;
So I, being young, till now ripe not* to reason.   *have not ripened*
125   And touching* now the point of human skill,*   *reaching | judgment*
Reason becomes the marshal to my will
And leads me to your eyes, where I o'erlook
Love's stories written in love's richest book.

HELENA   Wherefore was I to this keen mockery born?
130   When at your hands did I deserve this scorn?
Is't not enough, is't not enough, young man,
That I did never, no, nor never can,
Deserve a sweet look from Demetrius' eye,
But you must flout my insufficiency?
135   Good troth,* you do me wrong, good sooth,* you do,   *Indeed | truth*
In such disdainful manner me to woo.
But fare you well. Perforce I must confess
I thought you lord of more true gentleness.
O, that a lady, of one man refused,
140   Should of another therefore be abused! [*She exits.*]

LYSANDER   She sees not Hermia. Hermia, sleep thou there,
And never mayst thou come Lysander near!
For as a surfeit of the sweetest things
The deepest loathing to the stomach brings,
145   Or as tie heresies that men do leave
Are hated most of those they did deceive,
So thou, my surfeit and my heresy,
Of all be hated, but the most of me!

And, all my powers, address your love and might
150 To honour Helen and to be her knight! [*He exits.*]

HERMIA   [*Awaking*] Help me, Lysander, help me! Do thy best
To pluck this crawling serpent from my breast!
Ay me, for pity! What a dream was here!
Lysander, look how I do quake with fear.
155 Methought a serpent ate my heart away,
And you sat smiling at his cruel prey.*   attack
Lysander! What, removed? Lysander! Lord!
What, out of hearing? Gone? No sound, no word?
Alack, where are you? Speak, an if you hear;
160 Speak, of all loves! I swoon almost with fear.
No? Then I well perceive you are not nigh.
Either death or you I'll find immediately.

[*She exits.*]

Act 3.

Scene 1.
The wood. Titania lying asleep

[*Enter Quince, Snug, Bottom, Flute, Snout, and Starveling.*]

BOTTOM   Are we all met?

QUINCE   Pat,* pat; and here's a marvels* convenient place   *Exactly | ("marvelously" meant)*
for our rehearsal. This green plot shall be our stage, this
hawthorn brake* our tiring-house,* and we will do it in action   *thicket | dressing room*
5   as we will do it before the duke.

BOTTOM   Peter Quince?

QUINCE   What sayest thou, bully* Bottom?   *good fellow*

BOTTOM   There are things in this comedy of Pyramus and
Thisby that will never please. First, Pyramus must draw a sword to
10   kill himself, which the ladies cannot abide. How answer you that?

SNOUT   By'r lakin,* a parlous* fear.   *By our lady | perilous*

STARVELING   I believe we must leave the killing out, when all is done.

BOTTOM   Not a whit: I have a device to make all well. Write me
a prologue, and let the prologue seem to say, we will do no harm with
15   our swords, and that Pyramus is not killed indeed; and, for the more
better assurance, tell them that I, Pyramus, am not Pyramus, but
Bottom the weaver. This will put them out of fear.

QUINCE   Well, we will have such a prologue, and it shall be written in
eight and six.

20   BOTTOM   No, make it two more; let it be written in eight and eight.

SNOUT   Will not the ladies be afeard of the lion?

STARVELING   I fear it, I promise you.

BOTTOM   Masters, you ought to consider with yourselves. To bring
in—God shield us!—a lion among ladies, is a most dreadful thing.
25   For there is not a more fearful wild-fowl than your lion living; and
we ought to look to 't.

SNOUT   Therefore another prologue must tell he is not a lion.

BOTTOM   Nay, you must name his name, and half his face must be
seen through the lion's neck, and he himself must speak through,
30   saying thus, or to the same defect*—"Ladies"—or "Fair-ladies—   ("effect" meant)
I would wish you"—or "I would request you"—or "I would entreat
you—not to fear, not to tremble: my life for yours. If you think I come
hither as a lion, it were pity of my life. No, I am no such thing. I am
a man as other men are." And there indeed let him name his name
35   and tell them plainly he is Snug the joiner.

QUINCE   Well, it shall be so. But there is two hard things; that is,
to bring the moonlight into a chamber; for, you know, Pyramus and
Thisby meet by moonlight.

SNOUT   Doth the moon shine that night we play our play?

40   BOTTOM   A calendar, a calendar! Look in the almanac; find out
moonshine, find out moonshine.

QUINCE   Yes, it doth shine that night.

BOTTOM   Why, then may you leave a casement of the great chamber
window, where we play, open, and the moon may shine in at the casement.

45   QUINCE   Ay; or else one must come in with a bush of thorns and
a lanthorn, and say he comes to disfigure,* or to present, the person   ("figure" meant)
of Moonshine. Then, there is another thing: we must have a wall
in the great chamber; for Pyramus and Thisby, says the story,
did talk through the chink of a wall.

SNOUT   You can never bring in a wall. What say you, Bottom?

BOTTOM   Some man or other must present Wall: and let him have
some plaster, or some loam, or some roughcast about him, to signify
wall; and let him hold his fingers thus, and through that cranny shall
Pyramus and Thisby whisper.

QUINCE   If that may be, then all is well. Come, sit down, every
mother's son, and rehearse your parts. Pyramus, you begin. When
you have spoken your speech, enter into that brake, and so every
one according to his cue.

[*Enter Puck.*]

PUCK   What hempen homespuns* have we swagg'ring here,
So near the cradle of the fairy queen?
What, a play toward!* I'll be an auditor;
An actor too, perhaps, if I see cause.

QUINCE   Speak, Pyramus. Thisby, stand forth.

BOTTOM, AS PYRAMUS   Thisby, the flowers of odious savors sweet—

QUINCE   Odors, odors.

BOTTOM, AS PYRAMUS   —odors savors sweet:
So hath thy breath, my dearest Thisby dear.
But hark, a voice! Stay thou but here awhile,
And by and by I will to thee appear. [*He exits.*]

PUCK   A stranger Pyramus than e'er played here. [*He exits.*]

FLUTE   Must I speak now?

QUINCE   Ay, marry, must you; for you must understand he goes but
to see a noise that he heard, and is to come again.

FLUTE, AS THISBY   Most radiant Pyramus, most lily-white of hue,
Of color like the red rose on triumphant brier,*

country bumpkins

in preparation

rose bush

67

Most brisky juvenal and eke* most lovely Jew,   *also*
As true as truest horse, that yet would never tire,
I'll meet thee, Pyramus, at Ninny's tomb.

QUINCE "Ninus' tomb," man. Why, you must not speak that yet.
80 That you answer to Pyramus. You speak all your part at once, cues
and all. Pyramus, enter. Your cue is past; it is "never tire."

FLUTE, AS THISBY O—as true as truest horse, that yet would never tire.

[*Reenter Puck, and Bottom with an ass's head.*]

BOTTOM, AS PYRAMUS If I were fair, Thisby, I were only thine.

QUINCE O monstrous! O strange! We are haunted. Pray, masters!
85 Fly, masters! Help!

[*Quince, Snug, Flute, Snout, and Starveling exit.*]

PUCK I'll follow you, I'll lead you about a round,*   *circle dance*
Through bog, through bush, through brake, through brier.
Sometime a horse I'll be, sometime a hound,
A hog, a headless bear, sometime a fire;
90 And neigh, and bark, and grunt, and roar, and burn,
Like horse, hound, hog, bear, fire, at every turn. [*He exits.*]

BOTTOM Why do they run away? This is a knavery of them to make
me afeard.

[*Reenter Snout.*]

SNOUT O Bottom, thou art changed! What do I see on thee?

95 BOTTOM What do you see? You see an ass head of your own, do you?

[*Snout exits. Reenter Quince.*]

QUINCE Bless thee, Bottom! Bless thee! Thou art translated.*   *transformed*
[*He exits.*]

2020   Marcel Drama

Metamorphosis of the bottom   69

2020

marcel Dzama

Bottom's music awakens the fairy queen

BOTTOM I see their knavery. This is to make an ass of me; to fright
me, if they could. But I will not stir from this place, do what they can.
I will walk up and down here, and I will sing, that they shall hear
I am not afraid.

100
[*Sings*] *The ouzel* cock so black of hue,*   *blackbird*
With orange-tawny bill,
The throstle with his note so true,*   *thrush*
The wren with little quill—

105 TITANIA [*Awaking*] What angel wakes me from my flow'ry bed?

BOTTOM [*Sings*] *The finch, the sparrow, and the lark,*
The plain-song cuckoo gray,
Whose note full many a man doth mark,
And dares not answer nay—
110 for, indeed, who would set his wit to so foolish a bird? Who
would give a bird the lie,* though he cry "cuckoo" never so?* *contradict / ever so often*

TITANIA I pray thee, gentle mortal, sing again:
Mine ear is much enamored of thy note;
So is mine eye enthrallèd to thy shape;
115 And thy fair virtue's force perforce doth move me
On the first view to say, to swear, I love thee.

BOTTOM Methinks, mistress, you should have little reason for that.
And yet, to say the truth, reason and love keep little company together
nowadays; the more the pity that some honest neighbors will not
120 make them friends. Nay, I can gleek* upon occasion.   *make a joke*

TITANIA Thou art as wise as thou art beautiful.

BOTTOM Not so, neither; but if I had wit enough to get out of this
wood, I have enough to serve mine own turn.

TITANIA Out of this wood do not desire to go.
125 Thou shalt remain here, whether thou wilt or no.
I am a spirit of no common rate.*   *rank*
The summer still doth tend upon my state;
And I do love thee. Therefore, go with me.

2020

marcel Dzama

Thou art as wise as thou art beautiful

I'll give thee fairies to attend on thee,
130 And they shall fetch thee jewels from the deep,
And sing while thou on pressèd flowers dost sleep.
And I will purge thy mortal grossness so
That thou shalt like an airy spirit go.
Peaseblossom! Cobweb! Moth! And Mustardseed!

[*Enter Peaseblossom, Cobweb, Moth, and Mustardseed.*]

135 PEASEBLOSSOM   Ready.

COBWEB   And I.

MOTH   And I.

MUSTARDSEED   And I.

ALL   Where shall we go?

140 TITANIA   Be kind and courteous to this gentleman;
Hop in his walks and gambol* in his eyes;   *skip about*
Feed him with apricocks and dewberries,*   *apricots and blackberries*
With purple grapes, green figs, and mulberries;
The honey-bags steal from the humble-bees,
145 And for night-tapers crop their waxen thighs
And light them at the fiery glowworm's eyes,
To have my love to bed and to arise;
And pluck the wings from painted butterflies
To fan the moonbeams from his sleeping eyes.
150 Nod to him, elves, and do him courtesies.

PEASEBLOSSOM   Hail, mortal!

COBWEB   Hail!

MOTH   Hail!

MUSTARDSEED   Hail!

BOTTOM   I cry your worship's mercy,* hcartily: I beseech *beg your pardon*
your worship's name.

COBWEB   Cobweb.

BOTTOM   I shall desire you of more acquaintance, good
Master Cobweb: if I cut my finger, I shall make bold with you.*   *(cobweb used to stop bleeding)*
160   Your name, honest gentleman?

PEASEBLOSSOM   Peaseblossom.

BOTTOM   I pray you, commend me to Mistress Squash, your mother,
and to Master Peascod, your father. Good Master Peaseblossom, I shall
desire you of more acquaintance too. Your name, I beseech you, sir?

165   MUSTARDSEED   Mustardseed.

BOTTOM   Good Master Mustardseed, I know your patience
well. That same cowardly, giantlike ox-beef hath devoured*   *(mustard was condiment for beef)*
many a gentleman of your house. I promise you your kindred
had made my eyes water ere now. I desire you of more
170   acquaintance, good Master Mustardseed.

TITANIA   Come, wait upon him; lead him to my bower.
The moon methinks looks with a wat'ry eye;
And when she weeps, weeps every little flower,
Lamenting some enforcèd* chastity.   *assaulted*
175   Tie up my lover's tongue, bring him silently.

[*They exit.*]

74

Her mischievous messengers

Scene 2.
Another part of the wood

[*Enter Oberon.*]

OBERON   I wonder if Titania be awaked;
Then, what it was that next came in her eye,
Which she must dote on in extremity.*   *to the extreme*
[*Enter Puck.*]
Here comes my messenger. How now, mad spirit!
5   What night-rule* now about this haunted* grove?   *happenings | much visited*

PUCK   My mistress with a monster is in love.
Near to her close and consecrated bower,
While she was in her dull and sleeping hour,
A crew of patches,* rude mechanicals,*   *fools | uncivilized workers*
10   That work for bread upon Athenian stalls,
Were met together to rehearse a play
Intended for great Theseus' nuptial day.
The shallowest thick-skin of that barren sort,*   *dull drama*
Who Pyramus presented, in their sport,
15   Forsook his scene and entered in a brake.
When I did him at this advantage take,
An ass's nole* I fixèd on his head: *head*
Anon his Thisby must be answerèd,
And forth my mimic comes. When they him spy,
20   As wild geese that the creeping fowler* eye,   *hunter of wild birds*
Or russet-pated choughs, many in sort,*   *flock of brownish-headed jackdaws*
Rising and cawing at the gun's report,
Sever themselves and madly sweep the sky,
So, at his sight, away his fellows fly;
25   And, at our stamp, here o'er and o'er one falls;
He murder cries and help from Athens calls.
Their sense thus weak, lost with their fears thus strong,

Made senseless things begin to do them wrong;
For briers and thorns at their apparel snatch;
30 Some sleeves, some hats, from yielders all things catch.
I led them on in this distracted fear,
And left sweet Pyramus translated there:
When in that moment, so it came to pass,
Titania waked and straightway loved an ass.

35 OBERON   This falls out better than I could devise.
But hast thou yet latched the Athenian's eyes
With the love juice, as I did bid thee do?

PUCK   I took him sleeping—that is finished too—
And the Athenian woman by his side;
40 That, when he waked, of force* she must be eyed.   *by necessity*

[*Enter Hemia and Demetrius.*]

OBERON   Stand close:* this is the same Athenian.   *hidden*

PUCK   This is the woman, but not this the man.

DEMETRIUS   O, why rebuke you him that loves you so?
Lay breath so bitter on your bitter foe.

45 HERMIA   Now I but chide; but I should use thee worse,
For thou, I fear, hast given me cause to curse.
If thou hast slain Lysander in his sleep,
Being o'er shoes in blood, plunge in the deep,
And kill me too.
50 The sun was not so true unto the day
As he to me. Would he have stolen away
From sleeping Hermia? I'll believe as soon
This whole* earth may be bored* and that the moon   *solid | pierced*
May through the center creep and so displease
55 Her brother's* noontide with th' Antipodes.*   *the sun | the other side of the earth*
It cannot be but thou hast murdered him;
So should a murderer look, so dead,* so grim.   *pale*

DEMETRIUS   So should the murdered look, and so should I,
Pierced through the heart with your stern cruelty.
60   Yet you, the murderer, look as bright, as clear,
As yonder Venus in her glimmering sphere.

HERMIA   What's this to my Lysander? Where is he?
Ah, good Demetrius, wilt thou give him me?

DEMETRIUS   I had rather give his carcass to my hounds.

65   HERMIA   Out, dog! Out, cur! Thou driv'st me past the bounds
Of maiden's patience. Hast thou slain him, then?
Henceforth be never numbered among men!
O, once tell true! Tell true, even for my sake!
Durst thou have looked upon him being awake?
70   And hast thou killed him sleeping? O brave touch!
Could not a worm, an adder,* do so much?   *viper*
An adder did it; for with doubler tongue
Than thine, thou serpent, never adder stung.

DEMETRIUS   You spend your passion on a misprised mood:*   *mistaken anger*
75   I am not guilty of Lysander's blood;
Nor is he dead, for aught that I can tell.

HERMIA   I pray thee, tell me then that he is well.

DEMETRIUS   An if I could, what should I get therefore?

HERMIA   A privilege never to see me more.
80   And from thy hated presence part I so.
See me no more, whether he be dead or no. [*She exits.*]

DEMETRIUS   There is no following her in this fierce vein.
Here therefore for a while I will remain.
So sorrow's heaviness doth heavier grow
85   For debt that bankrout sleep doth sorrow owe;
Which now in some slight measure it will pay,
If for his tender* here I make some stay. [*Lies down and sleeps.*]   *offer*

OBERON   What hast thou done? Thou hast mistaken quite
And laid the love-juice on some true-love's sight:
90   Of thy misprision* must perforce* ensue   *mistake / necessarily*
Some true love turned, and not a false turned true.

PUCK   Then fate o'errules, that, one man holding troth,
A million fail, confounding* oath on oath.   *breaking*

OBERON   About the wood go swifter than the wind,
95   And Helena of Athens look thou find.
All fancy-sick* she is and pale of cheer,*   *lovesick / face*
With sighs of love, that costs the fresh blood dear:
By some illusion see thou bring her here.
I'll charm his eyes against* she do appear.   *to prepare for when*

100 PUCK   I go, I go; look how I go,
Swifter than arrow from the Tartar's bow. [*He exits.*]

OBERON   Flower of this purple dye,
        Hit with Cupid's archery,
        Sink in apple of his eye.
105   When his love he doth espy,
        Let her shine as gloriously
        As the Venus of the sky.
        When thou wakest, if she be by,
        Beg of her for remedy.

[*Reenter Puck.*]

110 PUCK   Captain of our fairy band,
Helena is here at hand;
And the youth, mistook by me,
Pleading for a lover's fee.
Shall we their fond pageant* see?   *foolish exhibition*
115 Lord, what fools these mortals be!

OBERON   Stand aside. The noise they make
Will cause Demetrius to awake.

PUCK   Then will two at once woo onc;
That must needs be sport alone;*   *unrivaled*
120 And those things do best please me
That befall prepost'rously.

[*Enter Lysander and Helena.*]

LYSANDER   Why should you think that I should woo in scorn?
Scorn and derision never come in tears:
Look, when I vow, I weep; and vows so born,
125 In their nativity all truth appears.
How can these things in me seem scorn to you,
Bearing the badge of faith,* to prove them true?   *his tears*

HELENA   You do advance* your cunning more and more.   *display*
When truth kills truth, O devilish-holy fray!
130 These vows are Hermia's: will you give her o'er?
Weigh oath with oath, and you will nothing weigh.
Your vows to her and me, put in two scales,
Will even weigh, and both as light as tales.

LYSANDER   I had no judgment when to her I swore.

135 HELENA   Nor none, in my mind, now you give her o'er.

LYSANDER   Demetrius loves her, and he loves not you.

DEMETRIUS   [*Awaking*] O Helen, goddess, nymph, perfect, divine!
To what, my love, shall I compare thine eyne?
Crystal is muddy. O, how ripe in show*   *appearance*
140 Thy lips, those kissing cherries, tempting grow!
That pure congealèd white, high Taurus' snow,
Fanned with the eastern wind, turns to a crow
When thou hold'st up thy hand: O, let me kiss
This princess of pure white, this seal of bliss!

145 HELENA   O spite! O hell! I see you all are bent
To set against me for your merriment:

If you were civil and knew courtesy,
You would not do me thus much injury.
Can you not hate me, as I know you do,
150 But you must join in souls to mock me too?
If you were men, as men you are in show,
You would not use a gentle lady so;
To vow, and swear, and superpraise my parts,*   *qualities
When I am sure you hate me with your hearts.
155 You both are rivals, and love Hermia;
And now both rivals to mock Helena:
A trim* exploit, a manly enterprise,   *fine (ironically)
To conjure tears up in a poor maid's eyes
With your derision! None of noble sort
160 Would so offend a virgin and extort*   *wring out
A poor soul's patience, all to make you sport.

LYSANDER   You are unkind, Demetrius. Be not so;
For you love Hermia; this you know I know:
And here, with all good will, with all my heart,
165 In Hermia's love I yield you up my part;
And yours of Helena to me bequeath,
Whom I do love and will do till my death.

HELENA   Never did mockers waste more idle breath.

DEMETRIUS   Lysander, keep thy Hermia; I will none.
170 If e'er I loved her, all that love is gone.
My heart to her but as guest-wise sojourned,
And now to Helen is it home returned,
There to remain.

LYSANDER   Helen, it is not so.

175 DEMETRIUS   Disparage not the faith thou dost not know,
Lest, to thy peril, thou aby it dear.*   *pay for it dearly
Look, where thy love comes; yonder is thy dear.

[Enter Hermia.]

HERMIA   Dark night, that from the eye his* function takes,   *its*

The ear more quick of apprehension makes;

180 Wherein it doth impair the seeing sense,

It pays the hearing double recompense.

Thou art not by mine eye, Lysander, found;

Mine ear, I thank it, brought me to thy sound.

But why unkindly didst thou leave me so?

185 LYSANDER   Why should he stay, whom love doth press to go?

HERMIA   What love could press Lysander from my side?

LYSANDER   Lysander's love, that would not let him bide,

Fair Helena, who more engilds the night

Than all you fiery oes* and eyes of light.   *orbs*

190 Why seek'st thou me? Could not this make thee know,

The hate I bear thee made me leave thee so?

HERMIA   You speak not as you think: it cannot be.

HELENA   Lo, she is one of this confederacy!

Now I perceive they have conjoined all three

195 To fashion this false sport, in spite of me.

Injurious Hermia! Most ungrateful maid!

Have you conspired, have you with these contrived

To bait* me with this foul derision?   *torture*

Is all the counsel that we two have shared,

200 The sisters' vows, the hours that we have spent,

When we have chid the hasty-footed time

For parting us—O, is all forgot?

All school days' friendship, childhood innocence?

We, Hermia, like two artificial* gods,   *skillful*

205 Have with our needles created both one flower,

Both on one sampler, sitting on one cushion,

Both warbling of one song, both in one key,

As if our hands, our sides, voices, and minds,

Had been incorporate.* So we grow together,   *one body*

210 Like to a double cherry, seeming parted,

But yet an union in partition;

Two lovely berries molded on one stem;
So, with two seeming bodies, but one heart;
Two of the first, like coats in heraldry,
215 Due but to one and crownèd with one crest.
And will you rent* our ancient love asunder,   *rend*
To join with men in scorning your poor friend?
It is not friendly, 'tis not maidenly.
Our sex, as well as I, may chide you for it,
220 Though I alone do feel the injury.

HERMIA   I am amazèd at your passionate words.
I scorn you not. It seems that you scorn me.

HELENA   Have you not set Lysander, as in scorn,
To follow me and praise my eyes and face?
225 And made your other love, Demetrius,
Who even but now did spurn me with his foot,
To call me goddess, nymph, divine, and rare,
Precious, celestial? Wherefore speaks he this
To her he hates? And wherefore doth Lysander
230 Deny your love, so rich within his soul,
And tender* me, forsooth,* affection,   *offer | in truth*
But by your setting on, by your consent?
What thought I be not so in grace* as you,   *favor*
So hung upon with love, so fortunate,
235 But miserable most, to love unloved?
This you should pity rather than despise.

HERMIA   I understand not what you mean by this.

HELENA   Ay, do. Persever,* counterfeit sad* looks,   *Persevere | grave*
Make mouths upon me when I turn my back;
240 Wink each at other; hold the sweet jest up.
This sport, well carried, shall be chronicled.
If you have any pity, grace, or manners,
You would not make me such an argument.*   *subject of scorn*
But fare ye well. 'Tis partly my own fault,
245 Which death or absence soon shall remedy.

LYSANDER   Stay, gentle Helena; hear my excuse:
My love, my life, my soul, fair Helena!

HELENA   O excellent!

HERMIA   Sweet, do not scorn her so.

250   DEMETRIUS   If she cannot entreat, I can compel.

LYSANDER   Thou canst compel no more than she entreat.
Thy threats have no more strength than her weak prayers.
Helen, I love thee; by my life, I do.
I swear by that which I will lose for thee,
255   To prove him false that says I love thee not.

DEMETRIUS   I say I love thee more than he can do.

LYSANDER   If thou say so, withdraw, and prove it too.

DEMETRIUS   Quick, come!

HERMIA   Lysander, whereto tends all this?

260   LYSANDER   Away, you Ethiope!

DEMETRIUS   No, no; he'll
Seem to break loose; take on as you would follow,
But yet come not: you are a tame man, go!

LYSANDER   Hang off, thou cat, thou burr! Vile thing, let loose,
265   Or I will shake thee from me like a serpent!

HERMIA   Why are you grown so rude? What change is this?
Sweet love?

LYSANDER   Thy love! Out, tawny Tartar, out!
Out, loathèd med'cine! O, hated potion, hence!

HERMIA   Do you not jest?

HELENA   Yes, sooth;* and so do you.   *truly*

LYSANDER   Demetrius, I will keep my word* with thee.   *promise to fight*

DEMETRIUS   I would I had your bond, for I perceive
A weak bond holds you. I'll not trust your word.

LYSANDER   What, should I hurt her, strike her, kill her dead?
Although I hate her, I'll not harm her so.

HERMIA   What, can you do me greater harm than hate?
Hate me! Wherefore? O me! What news, my love!
Am not I Hermia? Are not you Lysander?
I am as fair now as I was erewhile.
Since night you loved me; yet since night you left me.
Why, then you left me—O, the gods forbid!—
In earnest, shall I say?

LYSANDER   Ay, by my life,
And never did desire to see thee more.
Therefore be out of hope, of question, of doubt;
Be certain, nothing truer, 'tis no jest
That I do hate thee and love Helena.

HERMIA   O me! You juggler! You canker blossom!
You thief of love! What, have you come by night
And stol'n my love's heart from him?

HELENA   Fine, i' faith!
Have you no modesty, no maiden shame,
No touch of bashfulness? What, will you tear
Impatient answers from my gentle tongue?
Fie, fie! You counterfeit, you puppet, you!

HERMIA   Puppet? Why so? Ay, that way goes the game.
Now I perceive that she hath made compare

Between our statures; she hath urged her height,
And with her personage, her tall personage,
Her height, forsooth, she hath prevailed with him.
And are you grown so high in his esteem
Because I am so dwarfish and so low?
How low am I, thou painted maypole? Speak!
How low am I? I am not yet so low
But that my nails can reach unto thine eyes.

HELENA   I pray you, though you mock me, gentlemen,
Let her not hurt me. I was never curst;*   *quarrelsome*
I have no gift at all in shrewishness;
I am a right maid* for my cowardice.   *a girl*
Let her not strike me. You perhaps may think,
Because she is something lower than myself,
That I can match her.

HERMIA   Lower! Hark, again!

HELENA   Good Hermia, do not be so bitter with me.
I evermore did love you, Hermia,
Did ever keep your counsels, never wronged you;
Save that, in love unto Demetrius,
I told him of your stealth unto this wood.
He followed you; for love I followed him.
But he hath chid me hence and threatened me
To strike me, spurn me, nay, to kill me too:
And now, so you will let me quiet go,
To Athens will I bear my folly back
And follow you no further. Let me go.
You see how simple and how fond* I am.   *foolish*

HERMIA   Why, get you gone. Who is't that hinders you?

HELENA   A foolish heart, that I leave here behind.

HERMIA   What, with Lysander?

330 HELENA   With Demetrius.

LYSANDER   Be not afraid. She shall not harm thee, Helena.

DEMETRIUS   No, sir, she shall not, though you take her part.

HELENA   O, when she's angry, she is keen and shrewd!*   *cruel and shrewish
She was a vixen when she went to school;
335 And though she be but little, she is fierce.

HERMIA   "Little" again! Nothing but "low" and "little"!
Why will you suffer her to flout me thus?
Let me come to her.

LYSANDER   Get you gone, you dwarf;
340 You minimus,* of hind'ring knotgrass* made;   *smallest thing | weed
You bead, you acorn.

DEMETRIUS   You are too officious
In her behalf that scorns your services.
Let her alone. Speak not of Helena;
345 Take not her part; for, if thou dost intend
Never so little show of love to her,
Thou shalt aby* it.   *pay for

LYSANDER   Now she holds me not.
Now follow, if thou dar'st, to try whose right,
350 Of thine or mine, is most in Helena.

DEMETRIUS   Follow! Nay, I'll go with thee, cheek by jowl.

[*Lysander and Demetrius exit.*]

HERMIA   You, mistress, all this coil* is 'long of* you: *turmoil | because of
Nay, go not back.

HELENA   I will not trust you, I,
355 Nor longer stay in your curst company.

Your hands than mine are quicker for a fray,
My legs are longer though, to run away. [*She exits.*]

HERMIA   I am amazed, and know not what to say. [*She exits.*]

OBERON   This is thy negligence. Still thou mistak'st,
360 Or else committ'st thy knaveries willfully.

PUCK   Believe me, king of shadows, I mistook.
Did not you tell me I should know the man
By the Athenian garment he had on?
And so far blameless proves my enterprise,
365 That I have 'nointed an Athenian's eyes;
And so far am I glad it so did sort
As this their jangling I esteem a sport.

OBERON   Thou see'st these lovers seek a place to fight.
Hie* therefore, Robin, overcast the night;   *Hurry*
370 The starry welkin* cover thou anon   *sky*
With drooping fog as black as Acheron,
And lead these testy rivals so astray
As* one come not within another's way.   *That*
Like to Lysander sometime frame thy tongue,
375 Then stir Demetrius up with bitter wrong;
And sometime rail thou like Demetrius.
And from each other look thou lead them thus,
Till o'er their brows death-counterfeiting sleep
With leaden legs and batty* wings doth creep.   *batlike*
380 Then crush this herb into Lysander's eye;
Whose liquor hath this virtuous property,*   *potent power*
To take from thence all error with his might,
And make his eyeballs roll with wonted* sight.   *normal*
When they next wake, all this derision*   *delusion*
385 Shall seem a dream and fruitless vision,
And back to Athens shall the lovers wend,
With league whose date* till death shall never end.   *duration*
Whiles I in this affair do thee employ,
I'll to my queen and beg her Indian boy;

390 And then I will her charmèd eye release
From monster's view, and all things shall be peace.

PUCK   My fairy lord, this must be done with haste,
For night's swift dragons cut the clouds full fast,
And yonder shines Aurora's harbinger;*   *the morning star*
395 At whose approach, ghosts, wand'ring here and there,
Troop home to churchyards: damnèd spirits all,
That in crossways and floods have burial,
Already to their wormy beds are gone.
For fear lest day should look their shames upon,
400 They willfully themselves exile from light
And must for aye consort with black-browed night.

OBERON   But we are spirits of another sort.
I with the morning's love* have oft made sport   *Aurora*
And, like a forester, the groves may tread,
405 Even till the eastern gate, all fiery-red,
Opening on Neptune with fair blessèd beams,
Turns into yellow gold his salt green streams.
But, notwithstanding, haste; make no delay.
We may effect this business yet ere day. [*He exits.*]

410 PUCK   Up and down, up and down,
        I will lead them up and down:
        I am feared in field and town:
        Goblin, lead them up and down.
        Here comes one.

[*Reenter Lysander.*]

415 LYSANDER   Where art thou, proud Demetrius? Speak thou now.

PUCK, IN DEMETRIUS' VOICE   Here, villain; drawn* and ready.   *with drawn sword*
Where art thou?

LYSANDER   I will be with thee straight.

89

PUCK, IN DEMETRIUS' VOICE   Follow me, then,
420 To plainer ground.

[*Lysander exits, as following the voice. Reenter Demetrius.*]

DEMETRIUS   Lysander! Speak again:
Thou runaway, thou coward, art thou fled?
Speak! In some bush? Where dost thou hide thy head?

PUCK, IN LYSANDER'S VOICE   Thou coward, art thou bragging to the stars,
425 Telling the bushes that thou look'st for wars,
And wilt not come? Come, recreant! Come, thou child!
I'll whip thee with a rod. He is defiled
That draws a sword on thee.

DEMETRIUS   Yea, art thou there?

430 PUCK, IN LYSANDER'S VOICE   Follow my voice. We'll try no manhood*   *not test courage
      here.

[*They exit. Reenter Lysander.*]

LYSANDER   He goes before me and still dares me on:
When I come where he calls, then he is gone.
The villain is much lighter-heeled than I.
I followed fast, but faster he did fly;
435 That fallen am I in dark uneven way,
And here will rest me. Come, thou gentle day!
For if but once thou show me thy gray light,
I'll find Demetrius and revenge this spite. [*He lies down and sleeps.*]

[*Reenter Puck and Demetrius.*]

PUCK, IN LYSANDER'S VOICE   Ho, ho, ho! Coward, why com'st thou not?

440 DEMETRIUS   Abide me,* if thou dar'st; for well I wot*   *Wait for me / know
Thou runn'st before me, shifting every place,
And dar'st not stand, nor look me in the face.
Where art thou now?

Look me in the face. Where art thou?

2020

marcel DZAMA

Lost in the moonlight

PUCK, IN LYSANDER'S VOICE   Come hither. I am here.

445   DEMETRIUS   Nay, then, thou mock'st me. Thou shalt buy this dear,*   *pay dearly for this*
      If ever I thy face by daylight see.
      Now, go thy way. Faintness constraineth me
      To measure out my length on this cold bed.
      By day's approach look to be visited. [*He lies down and sleeps.*]

[*Reenter Helena.*]

450   HELENA   O weary night, O long and tedious night,
      Abate* thy hours! Shine comforts from the east,   *Make shorter*
      That I may back to Athens by daylight,
      From these that my poor company detest:
      And sleep, that sometimes shuts up sorrow's eye,
455   Steal me awhile from mine own company. [*She lies down and sleeps.*]

      PUCK   Yet but three? Come one more.
         Two of both kinds make up four.
         Here she comes, curst* and sad: *angry*
         Cupid is a knavish lad,
460   Thus to make poor females mad.

[*Reenter Hermia.*]

      HERMIA   Never so weary, never so in woe,
      Bedabbled with the dew and torn with briers,
      I can no further crawl, no further go;
      My legs can keep no pace with my desires.
465   Here will I rest me till the break of day.
      Heavens shield Lysander, if they mean a fray! [*She lies down and sleeps.*]

      PUCK   On the ground
         Sleep sound:
         I'll apply
470   To your eye,
      Gentle lover, remedy.
      [*Squeezes the juice on Lysander's eyes.*]

93

When thou wak'st,
Thou tak'st
True delight
475 In the sight
Of thy former lady's eye:
And the country proverb known,
That every man should take his own,
In your waking shall be shown.
480 Jack shall have Jill;
Nought shall go ill;
The man shall have his mare again, and all shall be well.

[*He exits.*]

Act 4.

Scene 1.
The same. Lysander, Demetrius, Hermia, and Helena lying asleep

[*Enter Titania and Bottom; Peaseblossom, Cobweb, Moth, Mustardseed, and other Fairies attending; Oberon behind, unseen.*]

TITANIA   Come, sit thee down upon this flow'ry bed,
While I thy amiable* cheeks do coy,*   *lovely | caress*
And stick musk-roses in thy sleek smooth head,
And kiss thy fair large ears, my gentle joy.

5   BOTTOM   Where's Peaseblossom?

PEASEBLOSSOM   Ready.

BOTTOM   Scratch my head, Peaseblossom. Where's Monsieur Cobweb?

COBWEB   Ready.

BOTTOM   Monsieur Cobweb, good monsieur, get you your weapons in
10   your hand, and kill me a red-hipped humble-bee on the top of a thistle;
and, good monsieur, bring me the honey-bag. Do not fret yourself
too much in the action, monsieur; and, good monsieur, have a care the
honey-bag break not; I would be loath to have you overflown with
a honey-bag, signior. Where's Monsieur Mustardseed?

15   MUSTARDSEED   Ready.

BOTTOM   Give me your neaf,* Monsieur Mustardseed. Pray you,   *fist*
leave your courtesy,* good monsieur.   *stop bowing*

MUSTARDSEED   What's your will?

I've only desire for you!

BOTTOM   Nothing, good monsieur, but to help Cavalery* Cobweb   *Cavalier*
to scratch. I must to the barber's, monsieur; for methinks I am
marvels* hairy about the face; and I am such a tender ass,   *("marvelously" meant)*
if my hair do but tickle me, I must scratch.

TITANIA   What, wilt thou hear some music, my sweet love?

BOTTOM   I have a reasonable good ear in music. Let's have the tongs
and the bones.*   *rustic music*

TITANIA   Or say, sweet love, what thou desirest to eat.

BOTTOM   Truly, a peck of provender.* I could munch your good dry   *hay*
oats. Methinks I have a great desire to a bottle of hay. Good hay,
sweet hay, hath no fellow.*   *equal*

TITANIA   I have a venturous fairy that shall seek
The squirrel's hoard, and fetch thee new nuts.

BOTTOM   I had rather have a handful or two of dried peas. But,
I pray you, let none of your people stir me: I have an exposition
of* sleep come upon me.   *("disposition for" meant)*

TITANIA   Sleep thou, and I will wind thee in my arms.
Fairies, begone, and be all ways away.
[*Fairies exit.*]
So doth the woodbine the sweet honeysuckle
Gently entwist; the female ivy so
Enrings the barky fingers of the elm.
O, how I love thee! How I dote on thee!

[*They sleep. Enter Puck.*]

OBERON   [*Advancing*] Welcome, good Robin. See'st thou
this sweet sight?
Her dotage now I do begin to pity:
For, meeting her of late behind the wood,
Seeking sweet favors from this hateful fool,

45 I did upbraid her and fall out with her.
    For she his hairy temples then had rounded
    With coronet of fresh and fragrant flowers;
    And that same dew, which sometime* on the buds   *formerly*
    Was wont to swell like round and orient* pearls,   *lustrous*
50 Stood now within the pretty flouriets' eyes,
    Like tears that did their own disgrace bewail.
    When I had at my pleasure taunted her
    And she in mild terms begged my patience,
    I then did ask of her her changeling child;
55 Which straight she gave me, and her fairy sent
    To bear him to my bower in fairy land.
    And now I have the boy, I will undo
    This hateful imperfection of her eyes:
    And, gentle Puck, take this transformèd scalp
60 From off the head of this Athenian swain,
    That, he awaking when the other* do,   *others*
    May all to Athens back again repair
    And think no more of this night's accidents*   *happenings*
    But as the fierce vexation of a dream.
65 But first I will release the fairy queen.
        Be as thou wast wont to be;
        See as thou wast wont to see.
        Dian's bud o'er Cupid's flower
        Hath such force and blessèd power.
70 Now, my Titania, wake you, my sweet queen.

TITANIA   My Oberon! What visions have I seen!
Methought I was enamoured of an ass.

OBERON   There lies your love.

TITANIA   How came these things to pass?
75 O, how mine eyes do loathe his visage now!

OBERON   Silence awhile. Robin, take off this head.
Titania, music call; and strike more dead
Than common sleep of all these five the sense.

2020   Marcel Deama

Restore and amend

101

TITANIA   Music, ho! Music, such as charmeth sleep!

80   PUCK   Now, when thou wak'st, with thine own fool's eyes peep.

OBERON   Sound, music! [*Music.*] Come, my queen, take hands with me,
And rock the ground whereon these sleepers be. [*They dance.*]
Now thou and I are new in amity,
And will tomorrow midnight solemnly*   *ceremoniously*
85   Dance in Duke Theseus' house triumphantly,*   *festively*
And bless it to all fair prosperity.
There shall the pairs of faithful lovers be
Wedded, with Theseus, all in jollity.

PUCK   Fairy king, attend, and mark:
90   I do hear the morning lark.

OBERON   Then, my queen, in silence sad,*   *serious*
Trip we after the night's shade.
We the globe can compass soon,
Swifter than the wand'ring moon.

95   TITANIA   Come, my lord, and in our flight
Tell me how it came this night
That I sleeping here was found
With these mortals on the ground.

[*Oberon, Titania, and Puck exit. Horns winded within.*
Enter Theseus, Hippolyta, Egeus, and train.]

THESEUS   Go, one of you, find out the forester,
100   For now our observation* is performed;   *observance of May Day rites*
And since we have the vaward* of the day,   *vanguard*
My love shall hear the music of my hounds.
Uncouple in the western valley; let them go.
Dispatch, I say, and find the forester.
[*Exit an attendant.*]
105   We will, fair queen, up to the mountain's top,
And mark the musical confusion
Of hounds and echo in conjunction.

HIPPOLYTA   I was with Hercules and Cadmus once,
When in a wood of Crete they bayed* the bear   *brought to bay
110 With hounds of Sparta. Never did I hear
Such gallant chiding; for, besides the groves,
The skies, the fountains, every region near
Seemed all one mutual cry. I never heard
So musical a discord, such sweet thunder.

115 THESEUS   My hounds are bred out of the Spartan kind,
So flewed, so sanded,* and their heads are hung   *with hanging cheeks and sandy-colored
With ears that sweep away the morning dew;
Crook-kneed, and dew-lapped like Thessalian bulls;
Slow in pursuit, but matched in mouth like bells,
120 Each under each. A cry* more tunable*   *pack | tuneful
Was never holloed to, nor cheered with horn,
In Crete, in Sparta, nor in Thessaly.
Judge when you hear. But, soft!* What nymphs are these?   *stop

EGEUS   My lord, this is my daughter here asleep;
125 And this, Lysander; this Demetrius is;
This Helena, old Nedar's Helena:
I wonder of their being here together.

THESEUS   No doubt they rose up early to observe
The rite of May, and hearing our intent,
130 Came here in grace our solemnity.*   *in honor of our observance
But speak, Egeus. Is not this the day
That Hermia should give answer of her choice?

EGEUS   It is, my lord.

THESEUS   Go, bid the huntsmen wake them with their horns.
[*Horns and shouts within. Lysander, Demetrius, Helena, and Hermia
wake and start up.*]
135 Good morrow, friends. Saint Valentine is past:
Begin these woodbirds but to couple now?

LYSANDER   Pardon, my lord.

THESEUS   I pray you all, stand up.
I know you two are rival enemies.
140 How comes this gentle concord in the world,
That hatred is so far from jealousy,*   *suspicion*
To sleep by hate, and fear no enmity?

LYSANDER   My lord, I shall reply amazedly,*   *confusedly*
Half sleep, half waking: but as yet, I swear,
145 I cannot truly say how I came here.
But, as I think—for truly would I speak,
And now do I bethink me, so it is—
I came with Hermia hither. Our intent
Was to be gone from Athens, where we might,
150 Without* the peril of the Athenian law—   *Outside of*

EGEUS   Enough, enough, my lord; you have enough.
I beg the law, the law, upon his head.
They would have stol'n away; they would, Demetrius,
Thereby to have defeated you and me,
155 You of your wife and me of my consent,
Of my consent that she should be your wife.

DEMETRIUS   My lord, fair Helen told me of their stealth,
Of this their purpose hither to this wood,
And I in fury hither followed them,
160 Fair Helena in fancy following me.
But, my good lord, I wot* not by what power—   *know*
But by some power it is—my love to Hermia,
Melted as the snow, seems to me now
As the remembrance of an idle gaud*   *worthless trinket*
165 Which in my childhood I did dote upon;
And all the faith, the virtue* of my heart,   *power*
The object and the pleasure of mine eye,
Is only Helena. To her, my lord,
Was I betrothed ere I saw Hermia:
170 But, like in sickness, did I loathe this food;
But, as in health, come to my natural taste,
Now I do wish it, love it, long for it,
And will for evermore be true to it.

THESEUS   Fair lovers, you are fortunately met.
Of this discourse we more will hear anon.
Egeus, I will overbear your will,
For in the temple by and by with us
These couples shall eternally be knit.
And, for the morning now is something* worn,   *somewhat*
Our purposed hunting shall be set aside.
Away with us to Athens. Three and three,
We'll hold a feast in great solemnity.*   *ceremony*
Come, Hippolyta.

[*Theseus, Hippolyta, Egeus, and train exit.*]

DEMETRIUS   These things seem small and undistinguishable,
Like far-off mountains turnèd into clouds.

HERMIA   Methinks I see these things with parted eye,
When everything seems double.

HELENA   So methinks:
And I have found Demetrius like a jewel,
Mine own, and not mine own.

DEMETRIUS   Are you sure
That we are awake? It seems to me
That yet we sleep, we dream. Do not you think
The duke was here, and bid us follow him?

HERMIA   Yea, and my father.

HELENA   And Hippolyta.

LYSANDER   And he did bid us follow to the temple.

DEMETRIUS   Why, then, we are awake. Let's follow him
And by the way let us recount our dreams.

[*They exit.*]

2020

marcel DZAMA

In the midnight hour

BOTTOM   [*Awaking*] When my cue comes, call me, and I will answer.
My next is "Most fair Pyramus." Heigh-ho! Peter Quince! Flute, the
bellows-mender! Snout, the tinker! Starveling! God's my life, stolen
hence, and left me asleep! I have had a most rare vision. I have had
a dream, past the wit of man to say what dream it was. Man is but
205 an ass, if he go about* to expound this dream. Methought I was—   *try*
there is no man can tell what. Methought I was—and methought
I had—but man is but a patched fool if he will offer to say what
methought I had. The eye of man hath not heard, the ear of man hath
not seen, man's hand is not able to taste, his tongue to conceive,
210 nor his heart to report, what my dream was. I will get Peter Quince
to write a ballad of this dream. It shall be called "Bottom's Dream,"
because it hath no bottom; and I will sing it in the latter end of a play,
before the duke. Peradventure, to make it the more gracious, I shall
sing it at her* death.   *Thisby's*

[*He exits.*]

Scene 2.
Athens. Quince's house

[Enter Quince, Flute, Snout, and Starveling.]

QUINCE   Have you sent to Bottom's house ? Is he come home yet?

STARVELING   He cannot be heard of. Out of doubt he is transported.*   *carried off*

FLUTE   If he come not, then the play is marred. It goes not forward, doth it?

5   QUINCE   It is not possible: you have not a man in all Athens able to discharge* Pyramus but he.   *play*

FLUTE   No, he hath simply the best wit of any handicraft man in Athens.

QUINCE   Yea and the best person too; and he is a very paramour for a sweet voice.

10   FLUTE   You must say "paragon." A paramour is, God bless us, a thing of naught.*   *evil thing*

[Enter Snug.]

SNUG   Masters, the duke is coming from the temple, and there is two or three lords and ladies more married. If our sport had gone forward, we had all been made men.

15   FLUTE   O sweet bully Bottom! Thus hath he lost sixpence a day during his life. He could not have 'scaped sixpence a day: an the duke had not given him sixpence a day for playing Pyramus, I'll be hanged. He would have deserved it. Sixpence a day in Pyramus, or nothing.

2020

Marcel DIAMA

Funny heroes for a new mythology

[*Enter Bottom.*]

BOTTOM   Where are these lads? Where are these hearts?

20   QUINCE   Bottom! O most courageous day! O most happy hour!

BOTTOM   Masters, I am to discourse wonders: but ask me not what;
for if I tell you, I am no true Athenian. I will tell you everything, right
as it fell out.

QUINCE   Let us hear, sweet Bottom.

25   BOTTOM   Not a word of* me. All that I will tell you is that the duke   *from*
hath dined. Get your apparel together, good strings to your beards,
new ribbons to your pumps;* meet presently* at the palace; every man   *shoes | right away*
look o'er his part; for the short and the long is, our play is preferred.*   *recommended*
In any case, let Thisby have clean linen; and let not him that plays
30   the lion pare his nails, for they shall hang out for the lion's claws.
And, most dear actors, eat no onions nor garlic, for we are to utter
sweet breath, and I do not doubt but to hear them say, it is a sweet
comedy. No more words. Away! Go, away!

[*They exit.*]

Act 5.

Scene 1.
Athens. The palace of Theseus

[*Enter Theseus, Hippolyta, Philostrate, Lords, and Attendants.*]

HIPPOLYTA   'Tis strange, my Theseus, that these lovers speak of.

THESEUS   More strange than true: I never may believe
These antique* fables, nor these fairy toys.*   *ancient / tales of fairies*
Lovers and madmen have such seething brains,
5 Such shaping fantasies,* that apprehend   *imaginations*
More than cool reason ever comprehends.
The lunatic, the lover, and the poet
Are of imagination all compact.*   *composed*
One sees more devils than vast hell can hold,
10 That is, the madman. The lover, all as frantic,
Sees Helen's beauty in a brow of Egypt.*   *face of a gypsy*
The poet's eye, in fine frenzy rolling,
Doth glance from heaven to earth, from earth to heaven;
And as imagination bodies forth
15 The forms of things unknown, the poet's pen
Turns them to shapes and gives to airy nothing
A local habitation and a name.
Such tricks hath strong imagination,
That if it would but apprehend some joy,
20 It comprehends* some bringer of that joy;   *includes*
Or in the night, imagining some fear,
How easy is a bush supposed a bear!

HIPPOLYTA   But all the story of the night told over,
And all their minds transfigured so together,
25 More witnesseth than fancy's images
And grows to something of great constancy;*   *consistency*
But, howsoever, strange and admirable.*   *wonderful*

2020

mariel Dema

Romance, rest and relaxation

THESEUS   Here come the lovers, full of joy and mirth.
[*Enter Lysander, Demetrius, Hermia, and Helena.*]
Joy, gentle friends! Joy and fresh days of love
30 Accompany your hearts!

LYSANDER   More than to us
Wait in your royal walks, your board, your bed!

THESEUS   Come now, what masques, what dances shall we have,
To wear away this long age of three hours
35 Between our after-supper and bedtime?
Where is our usual manager of mirth?
What revels are in hand? Is there no play,
To ease the anguish of a torturing hour?
Call Philostrate.

40 PHILOSTRATE   Here, mighty Theseus.

THESEUS   Say, what abridgement* have you for this evening?   *entertainment*
What masque? What music? How shall we beguile
The lazy time, if not with some delight?

PHILOSTRATE   There is a brief* how many sports are ripe:*   *list / ready to be presented*
45 Make choice of which your highness will see first. [*Giving a paper.*]

THESEUS   [*Reads*] "The battle with the Centaurs, to be sung
By an Athenian eunuch to the harp."
We'll none of that. That have I told my love,
In glory of my kinsman Hercules.
50 "The riot of the tipsy Bacchanals,
Tearing the Thracian singer in their rage."
That is an old device;* and it was played   *show*
When I from Thebes came last a conqueror.
"The thrice three Muses mourning for the death
55 Of Learning, late deceased in beggary."
That is some satire, keen and critical,
Not sorting with* a nuptial ceremony.   *suited to*
"A tedious brief scene of young Pyramus

And his love Thisby; very tragical mirth."
60 Merry and tragical! Tedious and brief!
That is, hot ice and wondrous strange snow.
How shall we find the concord of this discord?

PHILOSTRATE   A play there is, my lord, some ten words long,
Which is as brief as I have known a play;
65 But by ten words, my lord, it is too long,
Which makes it tedious; for in all the play
There is not one word apt, one player fitted.
And tragical, my noble lord, it is,
For Pyramus therein doth kill himself.
70 Which, when I saw rehearsed, I must confess,
Made mine eyes water; but more merry tears
The passion of loud laughter never shed.

THESEUS   What are they that do play it?

PHILOSTRATE   Hard-handed men that work in Athens here,
75 Which never labored in their minds till now,
And now have toiled their unbreathed* memories   *unexercised*
With this same play, against* your nuptial.   *in preparation for*

THESEUS   And we will hear it.

PHILOSTRATE   No, my noble lord;
80 It is not for you: I have heard it over,
And it is nothing, nothing in the world;
Unless you can find sport in their intents,
Extremely stretched and conned* with cruel pain,   *memorized*
To do you service.

85 THESEUS   I will hear that play;
For never anything can be amiss,
When simpleness* and duty tender it.   *sincerity*
Go, bring them in: and take your places, ladies.

[*Exit Philostrate.*]

HIPPOLYTA   I love not to see wretchedness o'er charged*   *overburdened*
90 And duty in his* service perishing.   *its*

THESEUS   Why, gentle sweet, you shall see no such thing.

HIPPOLYTA   He says they can do nothing in this kind.

THESEUS   The kinder we, to give them thanks for nothing.
Our sport shall be to take what they mistake:
95 And what poor duty cannot do, noble respect
Takes it in might, not merit.
Where I have come, great clerks* have purposèd   *scholars*
To greet me with premeditated welcomes;
Where I have seen them shiver and look pale,
100 Make periods in the midst of sentences,
Throttle their practiced accent in their fears,
And in conclusion dumbly have broke off,
Not paying me a welcome. Trust me, sweet,
Out of this silence yet I picked a welcome;
105 And in the modesty of fearful duty
I read as much as from the rattling tongue
Of saucy and audacious eloquence.
Love, therefore, and tongue-tied simplicity
In least speak most, to my capacity.*   *to my understanding*

[*Reenter Philostrate.*]

110 PHILOSTRATE   So please your grace, the Prologue is addressed.*   *ready*

THESEUS   Let him approach.

[*Flourish of trumpets. Enter Quince for the Prologue.*]

PROLOGUE   If we offend, it is with our good will.
That you should think, we come not to offend,
But with good will. To show our simple skill,
115 That is the true beginning of our end.*   *aim*
Consider then we come but in despite.

2020

marcel DZAMA

A midsummer night's dream

We do not come as minding to content you,
Our true intent is. All for your delight
We are not here. That you should here repent you,
120 The actors are at hand, and by their show
You shall know all that you are like to know.

THESEUS   This fellow doth not stand upon points.*   *heed punctuation*

LYSANDER   He hath rid his prologue like a rough colt; he knows
not the stop.* A good moral, my lord. It is not enough to speak,   *punctuation mark*
125 but to speak true.

HIPPOLYTA   Indeed he hath played on his prologue like a child on
a recorder; a sound, but not in government.*   *control*

THESEUS   His speech was like a tangled chain; nothing impaired,
but all disordered. Who is next?

[*Enter Pyramus and Thisby, Wall, Moonshine, and Lion.*]

130 PROLOGUE   Gentles, perchance you wonder at this show;
But wonder on, till truth make all things plain.
This man is Pyramus, if you would know;
This beauteous lady Thisby is certain.
This man, with lime and roughcast, doth present
135 Wall, that vile Wall which did these lovers sunder;
And through Wall's chink, poor souls, they are content
To whisper. At the which let no man wonder.
This man, with lanthorn, dog, and bush of thorn,
Presenteth Moonshine; for, if you will know,
140 By moonshine did these lovers think no scorn
To meet at Ninus' tomb, there, there to woo.
This grisly beast, which Lion hight* by name,   *is called*
The trusty Thisby, coming first by night,
Did scare away, or rather did affright;
145 And, as she fled, her mantle she did fall,*   *drop*
Which Lion vile with bloody mouth did stain.
Anon comes Pyramus, sweet youth and tall,

And finds his trusty Thisby's mantle slain:
Whereat, with blade, with bloody blameful blade,
150 He bravely broached* his boiling bloody breast; *stabbed*
And Thisby, tarrying in mulberry shade,
His dagger drew, and died. For all the rest,
Let Lion, Moonshine, Wall, and lovers twain
At large* discourse, while here they do remain. *At length*

[Prologue, Thisby, Lion, and Moonshine exit.]

155 THESEUS   I wonder if the lion be to speak.

DEMETRIUS   No wonder, my lord. One lion may, when many asses do.

WALL   In this same interlude it doth befall
That I, one Snout by name, present a wall;
And such a wall, as I would have you think,
160 That had in it a crannied hole or chink,
Through which the lovers, Pyramus and Thisby,
Did whisper often very secretly.
This loam, this roughcast, and this stone doth show
That I am that same wall; the truth is so:
165 And this the cranny is, right and sinister,* *left (horizontal)*
Through which the fearful lovers are to whisper.

THESEUS   Would you desire lime and hair to speak better?

DEMETRIUS   It is the wittiest* partition that ever I heard discourse, *most intelligent*
my lord.

[Enter Pyramus.]

170 THESEUS   Pyramus draws near the wall. Silence!

PYRAMUS   O grim-looked night! O night with hue so black!
O night, which ever art when day is not!
O night, O night! Alack, alack, alack,
I fear my Thisby's promise is forgot!

175 And thou, O wall, O sweet, O lovely wall,
That stand'st between her father's ground and mine!
Thou wall, O wall, O sweet and lovely wall,
Show me thy chink, to blink through with mine eyne!
[*Wall holds up his fingers.*]
Thanks, courteous wall. Jove shield thee well for this!
180 But what see I? No Thisby do I see.
O wicked wall, through whom I see no bliss!
Cursed be thy stones for thus deceiving me!

THESEUS The wall, methinks, being sensible,* should curse again.   *conscious*

PYRAMUS No, in truth, sir, he should not. "Deceiving me" is Thisby's
185 cue: she is to enter now, and I am to spy her through the wall. You shall
see, it will fall pat as I told you. Yonder she comes.

[*Enter Thisby.*]

THISBY O wall, full often hast thou heard my moans,
For parting my fair Pyramus and me!
My cherry lips have often kissed thy stones,
190 Thy stones with lime and hair knit up in thee.

PYRAMUS I see a voice: now will I to the chink,
To spy an I can hear my Thisby's face. Thisby!

THISBY My love thou art, my love I think.

PYRAMUS Think what thou wilt, I am thy lover's grace;
195 And, like Limander,* am I trusty still.   *(Leander meant)*

THISBY And I like Helen, till the Fates me kill.

PYRAMUS Not Shafalus to Procrus* was so true.   *(Cephalus and Procris, legendary lovers, meant)*

THISBY As Shafalus to Procrus, I to you.

PYRAMUS O kiss me through the hole of this vile wall!

200 THISBY   I kiss the wall's hole, not your lips at all.

PYRAMUS   Wilt thou at Ninny's tomb meet me straightway?

THISBY   'Tide life, 'tide death,* I come without delay.   *Come life or death*

[*Pyramus and Thisby exit.*]

WALL   Thus have I, Wall, my part dischargèd so;
And, being done, thus wall away doth go. [*He exits.*]

205 THESEUS   Now is the mural down between the two neighbors.

DEMETRIUS   No remedy, my lord, when walls are so willful to hear
without warning.

HIPPOLYTA   This is the silliest stuff that ever I heard.

THESEUS   The best in this kind are but shadows; and the worst are
210 no worse, if imagination amend them.

HIPPOLYTA   It must be your imagination then, and not theirs.

THESEUS   If we imagine no worse of them than they of themselves,
they may pass for excellent men. Here come two noble beasts in,
a man and a lion.

[*Enter Lion and Moonshine.*]

215 LION   You, ladies, you, whose gentle hearts do fear
The smallest monstrous mouse that creeps on floor,
May now perchance both quake and tremble here,
When lion rough in wildest rage doth roar.
Then know that I, as Snug the joiner, am
220 A lion fell,* nor else no lion's dam;*   *fierce / mother*
For, if I should as lion come in strife
Into this place, 'twere pity on my life.

122

THESEUS   A very gentle* beast, of a good conscience.   *courteous*

DEMETRIUS   The very best at a beast, my lord, that e'er I saw.

225   LYSANDER   This lion is a very fox for his valor.

THESEUS   True; and a goose for his discretion.

DEMETRIUS   Not so, my lord; for his valor cannot carry his discretion, and the fox carries the goose.

THESEUS   His discretion, I am sure, cannot carry his valor; for the
230   goose carries not the fox. It is well. Leave it to his discretion, and let us listen to the moon.

MOONSHINE   This lanthorn* doth the hornèd moon present—   *lantern*

DEMETRIUS   He should have worn the horns on his head.

THESEUS   He is no crescent, and his horns are invisible within
235   the circumference.

MOONSHINE   This lanthorn doth the hornèd moon present;
Myself the man i' th' moon do seem to be.

THESEUS   This is the greatest error of all the rest: the man should be put into the lanthorn. How is it else the man i' th' moon?

240   DEMETRIUS   He dares not come there for the candle; for, you see, it is already in snuff.*   *angry*

HIPPOLYTA   I am aweary of this moon. Would he would change!

THESEUS   It appears, by his small light of discretion, that he is in the wane; but yet, in courtesy, in all reason, we must stay the time.

245   LYSANDER   Proceed, Moon.

MOONSHINE   All that I have to say, is, to tell you that the lanthorn is the moon; I, the man i' th' moon; this thorn bush, my thorn bush; and this dog, my dog.

DEMETRIUS   Why, all these should be in the lanthorn; for all these
250   are in the moon. But, silence! Here comes Thisby.

[*Enter Thisby.*]

THISBY   This is old Ninny's tomb. Where is my love?

LION   [*Roaring*] Oh—

[*Thisby runs off.*]

DEMETRIUS   Well roared, Lion.

THESEUS   Well run, Thisby.

255   HIPPOLYTA   Well shone, Moon. Truly, the moon shines with a good grace.

[*The Lion shakes Thisby's mantle and exits.*]

THESEUS   Well moused,* Lion.   *shaken*

DEMETRIUS   And then came Pyramus.

LYSANDER   And so the lion vanished.

[*Enter Pyramus.*]

PYRAMUS   Sweet Moon, I thank thee for thy sunny beams;
260   I thank thee, Moon, for shining now so bright;
For, by thy gracious, golden, glittering gleams,
I trust to take of truest Thisby sight.
But stay, O spite!
But mark, poor knight,
265   What dreadful dole* is here!   *sorrow*

Eyes, do you see?
How can it be?
O dainty duck! O dear!
Thy mantle good,

270   What, stained with blood!
Approach, ye Furies fell!*   *fierce*
O Fates, come, come,
Cut thread and thrum;
Quail,* crush, conclude, and quell!*   *Destroy | kill*

275   THESEUS   This passion, and the death of a dear friend, would go
near to make a man look sad.

HIPPOLYTA   Beshrew* my heart, but I pity the man.   *Curse*

PYRAMUS   O wherefore, Nature, didst thou lions frame?
Since lion vile hath here deflowered* my dear: *("devoured" meant)*

280   Which is—no, no—which was the fairest dame
That lived, that loved, that liked, that looked with cheer.*   *countenance*
Come, tears, confound;
Out, sword, and wound
The pap* of Pyramus;   *breast*

285   Ay, that left pap,
Where heart doth hop. [*He stabs himself.*]
Thus die I, thus, thus, thus.
Now am I dead,
Now am I fled;

290   My soul is in the sky:
Tongue, lose thy light;
Moon take thy flight. [*Moonshine exits.*]
Now die, die, die, die, die. [*Pyramus dies.*]

DEMETRIUS   No die,* but an ace,* for him; for he is but one.   *(sing. of "dice") | one spot on a die*

295   LYSANDER   Less than an ace, man; for he is dead; he is nothing.

THESEUS   With the help of a surgeon he might yet recover, and
yet prove an ass.

Lion vile hath deflowered my dear

HIPPOLYTA   How chance Moonshine is gone before Thisby comes
back and finds her lover?

300   THESEUS   She will find him by starlight. Here she comes; and her
passion ends the play.

[*Reenter Thisby.*]

HIPPOLYTA   Methinks she should not use a long one for such
a Pyramus. I hope she will be brief.

DEMETRIUS   A mote will turn the balance, which Pyramus, which
305   Thisby, is the better; he for a man, God warrant us; she for a woman,
God bless us.

LYSANDER   She hath spied him already with those sweet eyes.

DEMETRIUS   And thus she means,* *videlicet*—   *laments | as follows*

THISBY   Asleep, my love?
310   What, dead, my dove?
O Pyramus, arise!
Speak, speak. Quite dumb?*   *silent*
Dead, dead? A tomb
Must cover thy sweet eyes.
315   These lily lips,
This cherry nose,
These yellow cowslip cheeks,
Are gone, are gone.
Lovers, make moan.
320   His eyes were green as leeks.
O Sisters Three,*   *the three Fates*
Come, come to me,
With hands as pale as milk;
Lay them in gore,
325   Since you have shore*   *shorn*
With shears his thread of silk.
Tongue, not a word:
Come, trusty sword;

Come, blade, my breast imbrue!* [*She stabs herself.*]   stain with blood

330 And, farewell, friends.
Thus Thisby ends.
Adieu, adieu, adieu. [*She dies.*]

THESEUS   Moonshine and Lion are left to bury the dead.

DEMETRIUS   Ay, and Wall too.

335 BOTTOM   [*Starting up*] No, I assure you; the wall is down that
parted their fathers. Will it please you to see the epilogue, or to hear
a Bergomask dance* between two of our company?   rustic dance

THESEUS   No epilogue, I pray you; for your play needs no excuse.
Never excuse, for when the players are all dead, there needs none to
340 be blamed. Marry, if he that writ it had played Pyramus and hanged
himself in Thisby's garter, it would have been a fine tragedy: and so
it is, truly; and very notably discharged. But come, your Bergomask.
Let your epilogue alone. [*A dance.*]
The iron tongue of midnight hath told twelve.
345 Lovers, to bed; 'tis almost fairy time.
I fear we shall outsleep the coming morn
As much as we this night have overwatched.
This palpable-gross* play hath well beguiled   obviously crude
The heavy gait of night. Sweet friends, to bed.
350 A fortnight hold we this solemnity,
In nightly revels and new jollity.

[*They exit. Enter Puck.*]

PUCK   Now the hungry lion roars,
And the wolf behowls the moon;
Whilst the heavy plowman snores,
355 All with weary task fordone.
Now the wasted brands* do glow,   burned logs
Whilst the screech-owl, screeching loud,
Puts the wretch that lies in woe
In remembrance of a shroud.

2020

marcel DZAMA

Life is a shipwreck but we must not forget to sing in the lifeboats

360 Now it is the time of night
That the graves all gaping wide,
Every one lets forth his sprite,
In the church-way paths to glide:
And we fairies, that do run
365 By the triple Hecate's team,
From the presence of the sun,
Following darkness like a dream,
Now are frolic.* Not a mouse   *frolicsome
Shall disturb this hallowed house:
370 I am sent with broom before,
To sweep the dust behind the door.

[*Enter Oberon and Titania with their train.*]

OBERON   Through the house give gathering light,
By the dead and drowsy fire:
Every elf and fairy sprite
375 Hop as light as bird from brier;
And this ditty, after me,
Sing, and dance it trippingly.

TITANIA   First, rehearse your song by rote,
To each word a warbling note:
380 Hand in hand, with fairy grace,
Will we sing, and bless this place. [*Song and dance.*]

OBERON   Now, until the break of day,
Through this house each fairy stray.
To the best bride-bed will we,
385 Which by us shall blessèd be;
And the issue there create
Ever shall be fortunate.
So shall all the couples three
Ever true in loving be;
390 And the blots of Nature's hand*   *deformities
Shall not in their issue stand.*   *appear in their offspring
Never mole, hare lip, nor scar,

Nor mark prodigious,* such as are   *ominous*
Despisèd in nativity,
395 Shall upon their children be.
With this field-dew consecrate,
Every fairy take his gait,
And each several* chamber bless,   *individual*
Through this palace, with sweet peace,
400 And the owner of it blest
Ever shall in safety rest.
Trip away; make no stay;
Meet me all by break of day.

[*Oberon, Titania, and train exit.*]

PUCK   If we shadows have offended,
405 Think but this, and all is mended:
That you have but slumbered here
While these visions did appear.
And this weak and idle* theme,   *foolish*
No more yielding but a dream,
410 Gentles, do not reprehend:
If you pardon, we will mend.
And, as I am an honest Puck,
If we have unearnèd luck
Now to 'scape the serpent's tongue,
415 We will make amends ere long;
Else the Puck a liar call.
So, good night unto you all.
Give me your hands,* if we be friends,   *Applaud*
And Robin shall restore amends.

[*He exits.*]

Thus ends the evening's entertainment

Nothin' ever ends

List
of Works

Asleep near the ocean, 2020
Watercolor, ink, and graphite on paper
12 ¼ × 9 inches
31.1 × 22.9 cm
Collection of Hyunkee Seong
p. 60

Bottom's music awakens the fairy queen,
2020
Watercolor, ink, and graphite on paper
12 ⅛ × 9 inches
30.8 × 22.9 cm
Philara Collection, Düsseldorf
p. 70

For Willem and Shelley, 2020
Watercolor, ink, and graphite on paper
8 ½ × 5 ½ inches
21.6 × 14 cm
p. 5

Funny heroes for a new mythology, 2020
Watercolor, ink, and graphite on paper
12 ¼ × 9 inches
31.1 × 22.9 cm
Collection of Yoosin Kim
p. 109

Her mischievous messengers, 2019
Gouache, ink, and graphite on paper
12 ¼ × 9 inches
31.1 × 22.9 cm
Collection of Yoosin Kim
p. 75

I know a flower of evil, 2020
Watercolor, ink, and graphite on paper
12 ¼ × 9 inches
31.1 × 22.9 cm
Collection of Aileen Getty
p. 54

I must be thy lady, 2020
Watercolor, ink, and graphite on paper
12 ⅛ × 9 inches
30.8 × 22.9 cm
p. 46

In the midnight hour, 2020
Watercolor, ink, and graphite on paper
12 ⅛ × 9 inches
30.8 × 22.9 cm
p. 106

I've only desire for you!, 2020
Watercolor, ink, and graphite on paper
12 ¼ × 9 inches
31.1 × 22.9 cm
Collection of Xiaohua Liu Family
p. 98

*Life is a shipwreck but we must not forget
to sing in the lifeboats*, 2020
Watercolor, ink, and graphite on paper
12 ⅛ × 9 inches
30.8 × 22.9 cm
p. 129

Lion vile hath deflowered my dear, 2020
Watercolor, ink, and graphite on paper
8 ½ × 5 ½ inches
21.6 × 14 cm
p. 126

Look me in the face. Where art thou?,
2020
Watercolor, ink, and graphite on paper
8 ½ × 5 ½ inches
21.6 × 14 cm
p. 91

Lost in the moonlight, 2020
Watercolor, ink, and graphite on paper
12 ⅛ × 9 inches
30.8 × 22.9 cm
p. 92

A mermaid on a dolphin's back, uttering harmonious breath, 2020
Watercolor, ink, and graphite on paper
12 ¼ × 9 inches
31.1 × 22.9 cm
Collection of Xi Tao
p. 51

The merrier hour was never wasted, 2020
Watercolor, ink, and graphite on paper
12 ⅛ × 9 inches
30.8 × 22.9 cm
Collection of Aileen Getty
p. 45

Metamorphosis of the bottom, 2020
Watercolor, ink, and graphite on paper
12 ¼ × 9 inches
31.1 × 22.9 cm
Collection of Aileen Getty
p. 69

A midsummer desire under moonlight,
2020
Watercolor, ink, and graphite on paper
12 ⅛ × 9 inches
30.8 × 22.9 cm
p. 26

A midsummer night's dream, 2019
Gouache, ink, and graphite on paper
12 ¼ × 9 inches
31.1 × 22.9 cm
Private collection, India
p. 118

Nothin' ever ends, 2020
Watercolor, ink, and graphite on paper
8 ½ × 5 ½ inches
21.6 × 14 cm
p. 135

Restore and amend, 2020
Watercolor, ink, and graphite on paper
12 ¼ × 9 inches
31.1 × 22.9 cm
Private collection
p. 101

Romance, rest and relaxation, 2020
Watercolor, ink, and graphite on paper
12 ¼ × 9 inches
31.1 × 22.9 cm
Collection of Witold Karalow
p. 114

Shakespeare, 2020
Watercolor, ink, and graphite on paper
8 ½ × 5 ½ inches
21.6 × 14 cm
p. 1

Sing me now asleep, 2020
Watercolor, ink, and graphite on paper
12 ⅛ × 9 inches
30.8 × 22.9 cm
p. 57

A song that rouses passions, 2020
Watercolor, ink, and graphite on paper
12 ¼ × 9 inches
31.1 × 22.9 cm
Collection of Aileen Getty
p. 34

Thou art as wise as thou art beautiful,
2020
Watercolor, ink, and graphite on paper
12 ⅛ × 9 inches
30.8 × 22.9 cm
Private collection, Sweden
p. 72

Thus ends the evening's entertainment,
2020
Watercolor, ink, and graphite on paper
8 ½ × 5 ½ inches
21.6 × 14 cm
Collection of Robert Levy, M.D.
p. 132

When rock becomes air, 2020
Watercolor, ink, and graphite on paper
12 ⅛ × 9 inches
30.8 × 22.9 cm
Private collection
p. 29

Acknowl-
edgments

David Zwirner wishes to thank Marcel Dzama, without whom this publication would not have been possible, as well as Julia Mechtler for her close collaboration and support.

Special thanks are due to Leslie Jamison for her thoughtful and compelling text. For their work on this publication, thank you to Rebecca Ashby-Colón, Claire Bidwell, Elizabeth Brannan-Williams, Andrea Brignolo, Kim Davidson, Joel Fennell, Joanna Fiorentino, Doro Globus, Elizabeth Gordon, Maris Hutchinson, Leann Li, Anna Mahony, Kerry McFate, Grace Munro, Clive Murphy, Katie Priest, Marc Sapir, Sarah Schrauwen, Molly Stein, Jules Thomson, Chandra Wohleber, and Lucas Zwirner.

A *Midsummer Night's Dream*
William Shakespeare × Marcel Dzama

From the series *Seeing Shakespeare*

David Zwirner Books
529 West 20th Street, 2nd Floor
New York, New York 10011
+1 212 727 2070
davidzwirnerbooks.com

Managing Director Doro Globus
Editorial Director Lucas Zwirner
Sales and Distribution Manager
Molly Stein

Project Editor Elizabeth Gordon
Proofreader Chandra Wohleber
Design Sarah Schrauwen
Production Manager Jules Thomson
Color Separations VeronaLibri, Verona
Printing VeronaLibri, Verona

Typeface Freight Text
Paper Multi Offset, 120 gsm

Publication © 2021 David Zwirner Books
"Sympathetic Magic" © 2021
Leslie Jamison
All artwork © 2021 Marcel Dzama

Photography
pp. 1, 5, 26, 29, 34, 45, 46, 51, 57,
70, 72, 75, 91, 92, 106, 109, 118, 126,
129, 132, 135: Kerry McFate
pp. 54, 69, 101: Maris Hutchinson
p. 60: Gana Art
p. 98: Kitmin Lee

Distributed in the United States
and Canada by
Simon & Schuster, Inc.
1230 Avenue of the Americas
New York, New York 10020
simonandschuster.com

Distributed outside the United States
and Canada by
Thames & Hudson, Ltd.
181A High Holborn
London WC1V 7QX
thamesandhudson.com

ISBN 978-1-64423-044-2
Library of Congress Control Number:
2020924253

Printed in Italy

Cover *Asleep near the ocean*, 2020 (detail)

A Note on the Text
This edition of *A Midsummer Night's
Dream* is based on the First Quarto of
1600. Spelling and punctuation have
been standardized, but certain forms of
words remain as in the original if they
sound distinctly different from modern
forms, such as *an* for *if*.